Mel Bay's
Mandolin Scales & Studies

By Ray Bell

2 3 4 5 6 7 8 9 0

Contents

This is a reference and practical exercise book of scales for the mandolin.

The first series of studies is based on a five-note scale called the pentatonic.

Pentatonic Scales

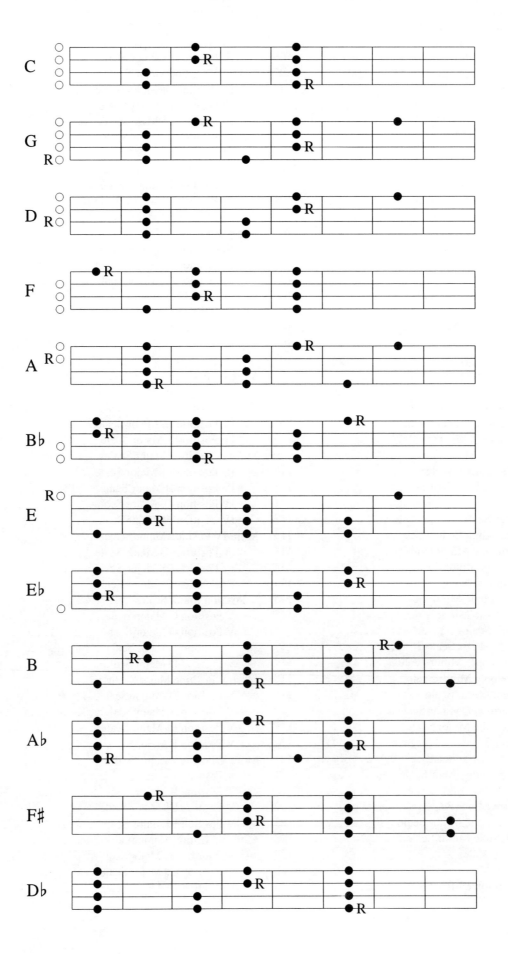

C Pentatonic Scale

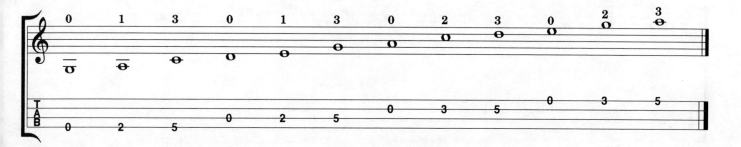

Exercise 1

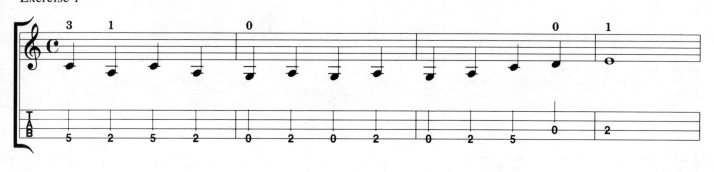

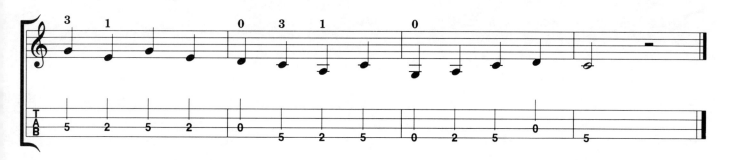

Exercise 2

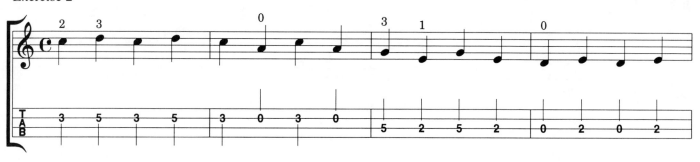

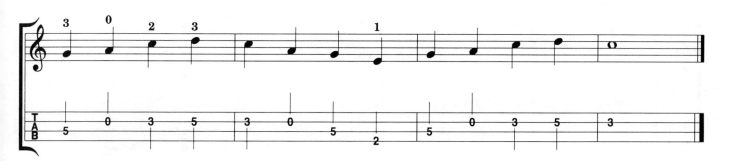

Exercise 3

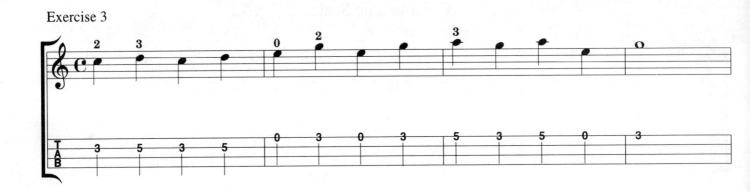

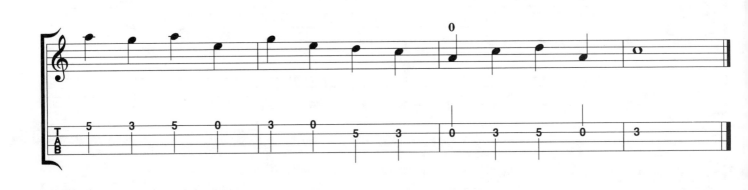

Exercise 4

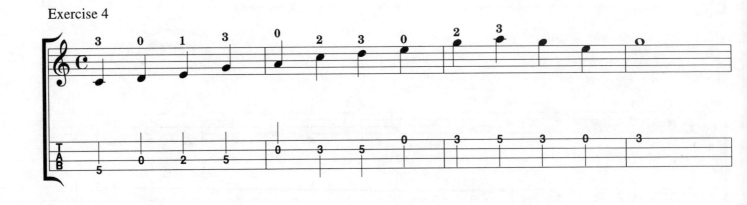

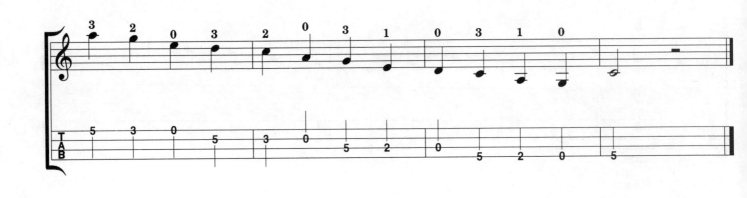

G Pentatonic Scale

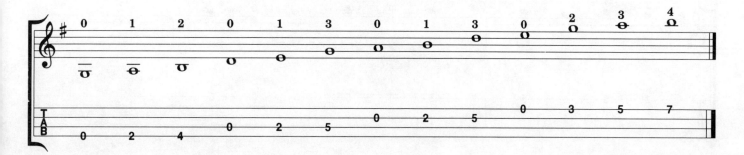

Exercise 1

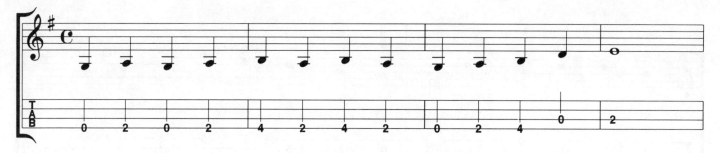

Exercise 2

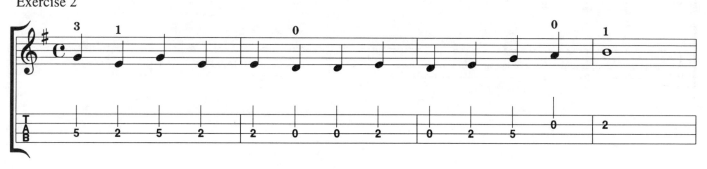

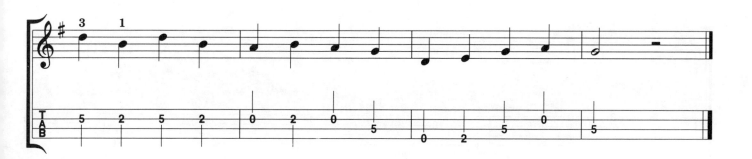

Exercise 3

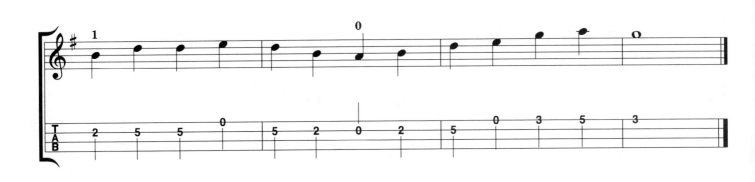

Exercise 4

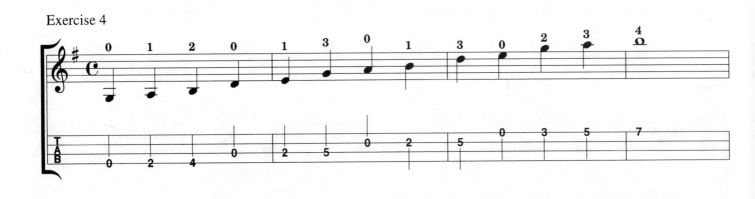

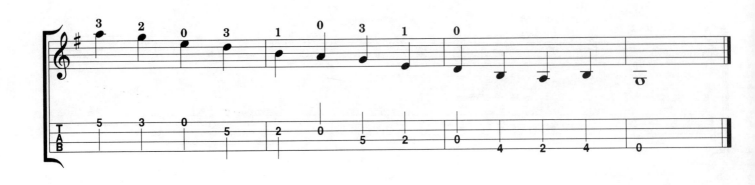

D Pentatonic Scale

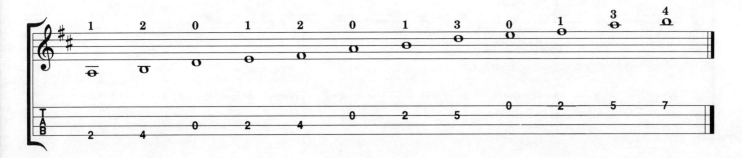

Exercise 1

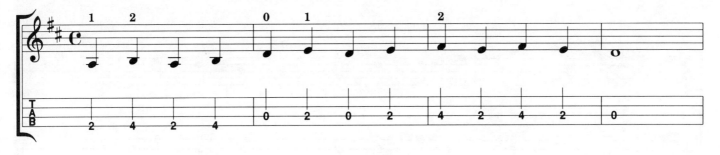

Exercise 2

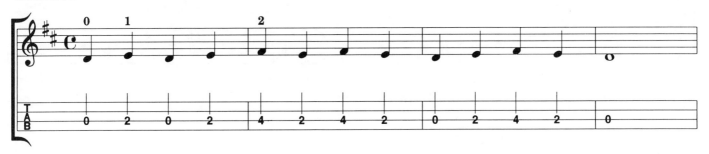

Exercise 3

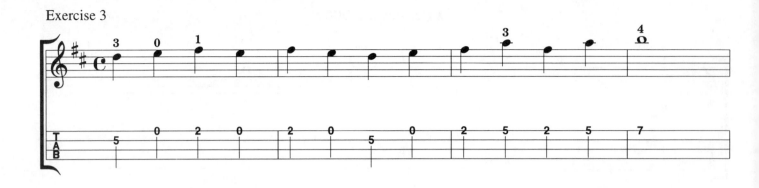

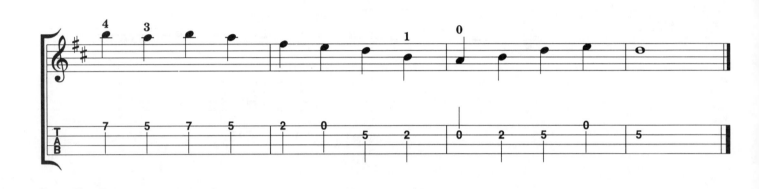

Exercise 4

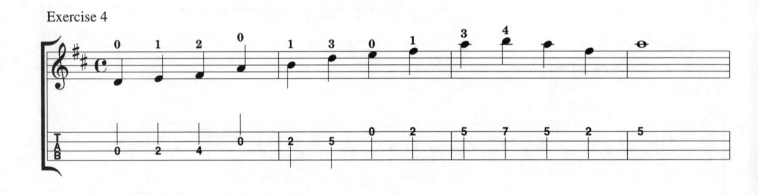

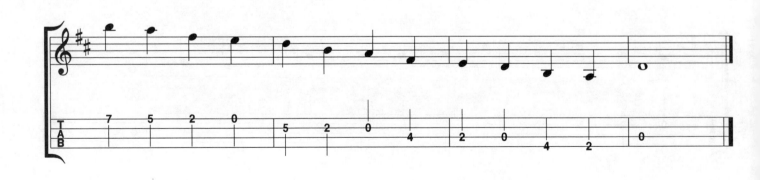

F Pentatonic Scale

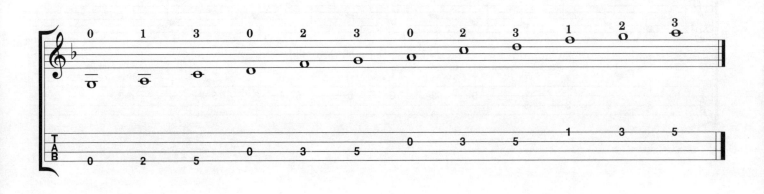

Exercise 1

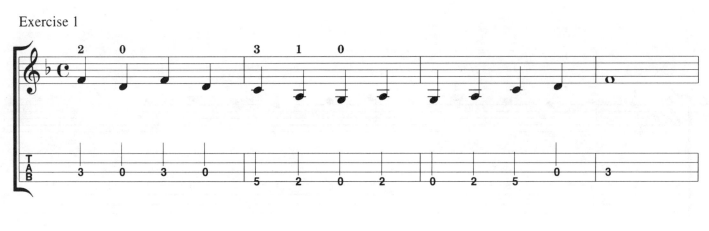

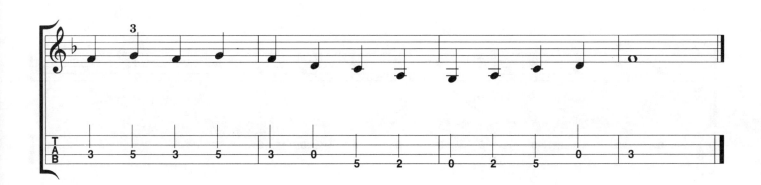

Exercise 2

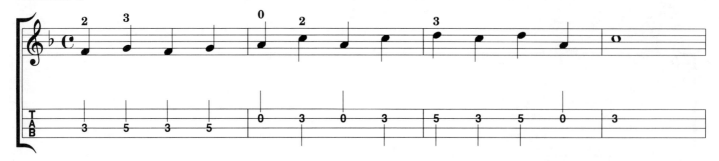

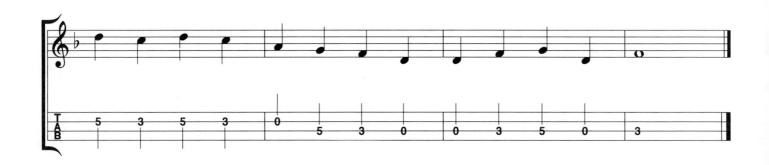

Exercise 3

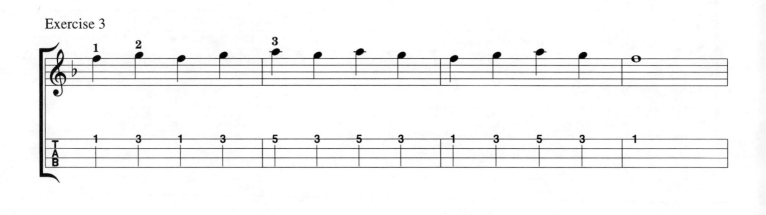

Exercise 4

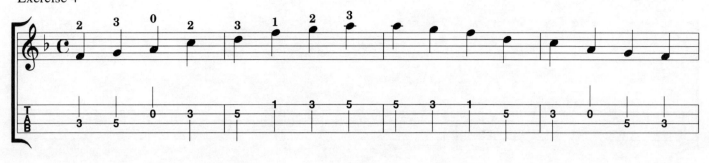

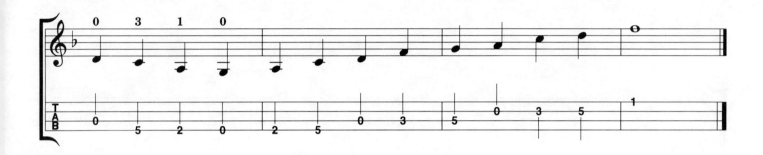

A Pentatonic Scale

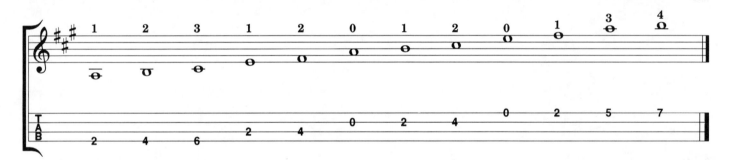

Exercise 1

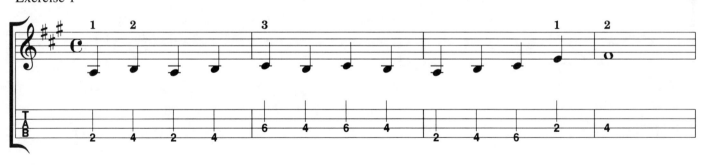

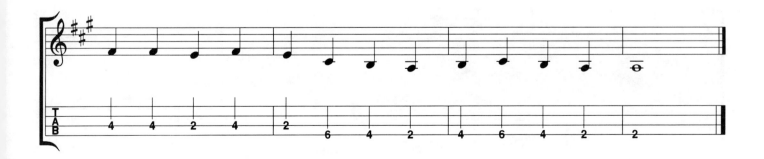

Exercise 2

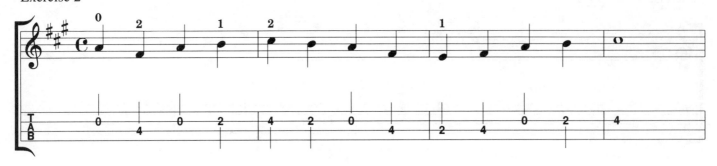

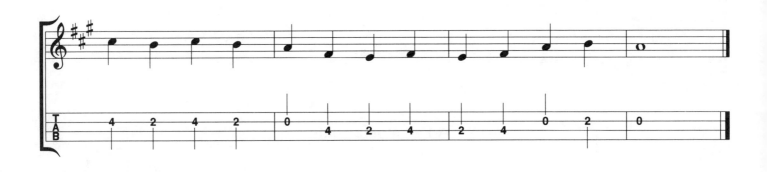

Exercise 3

Exercise 4

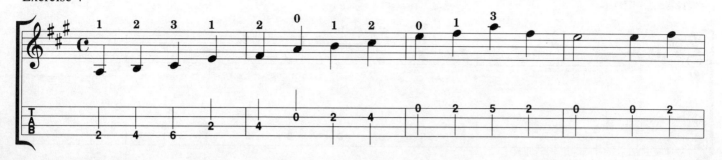

Bb Pentatonic Scale

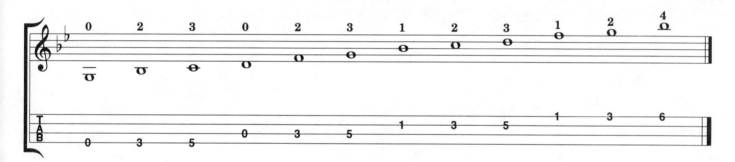

Exercise 1

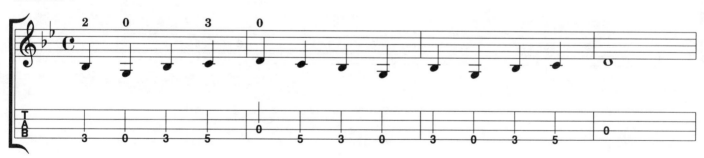

Exercise 2

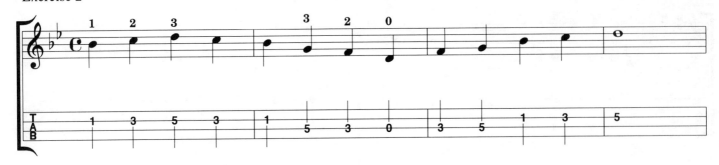

Exercise 3

Exercise 4

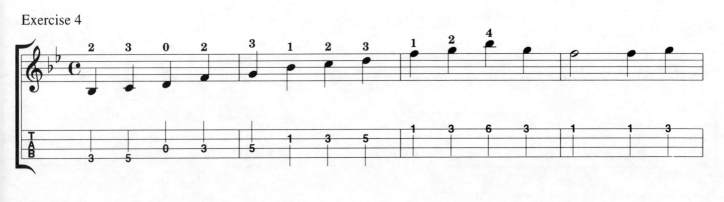

E Pentatonic Scale

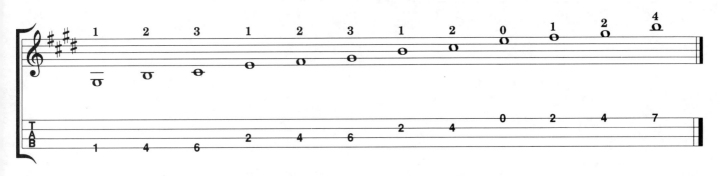

Exercise 1

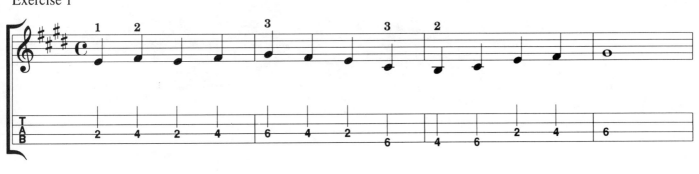

Exercise 2

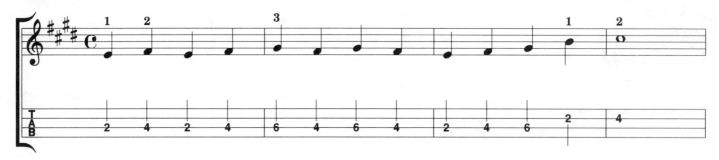

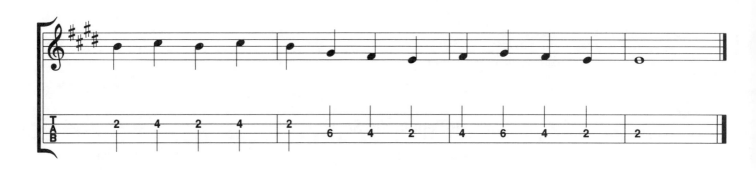

Exercise 3

Exercise 4

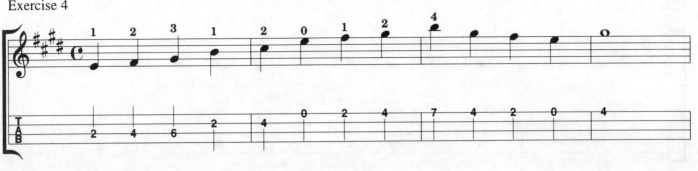

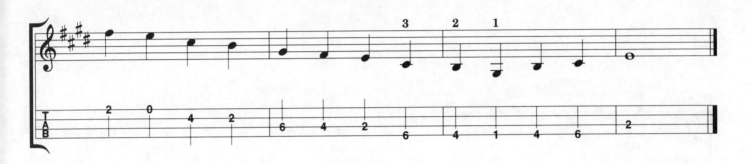

Eb Pentatonic Scale

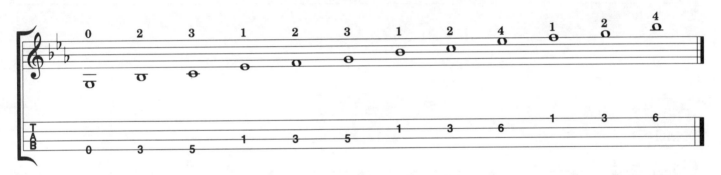

Exercise 1

Exercise 2

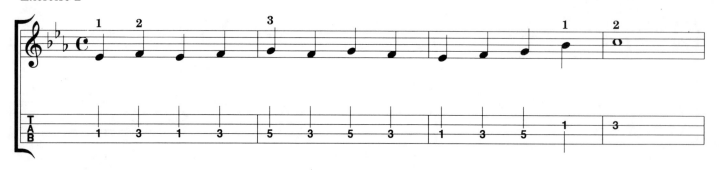

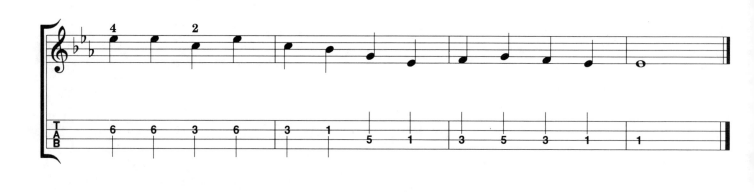

Exercise 3

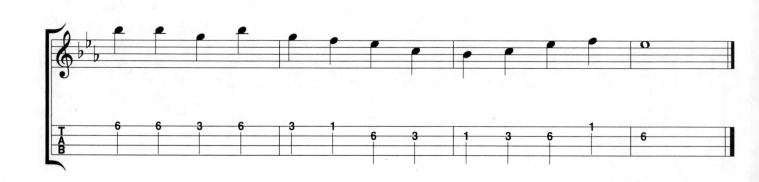

Exercise 4

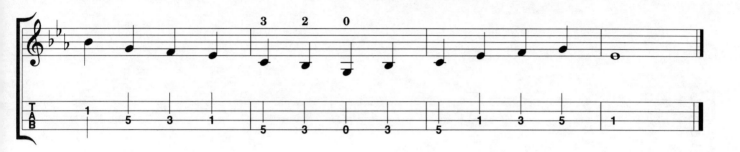

B Pentatonic Scale

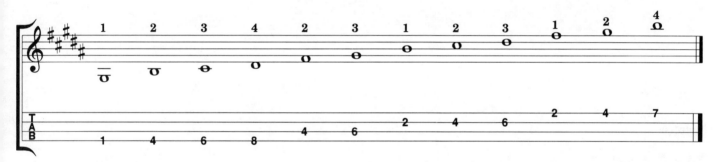

Exercise 1

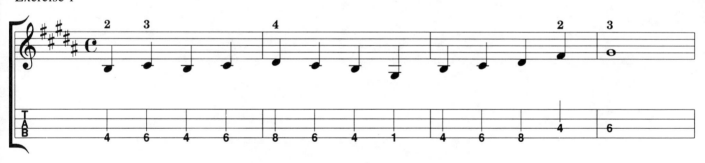

Exercise 2

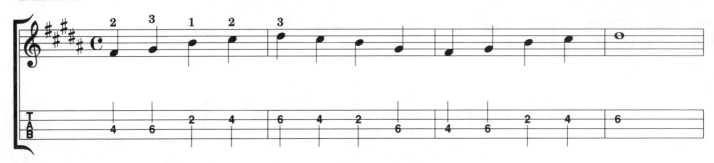

Exercise 3

22

Exercise 4

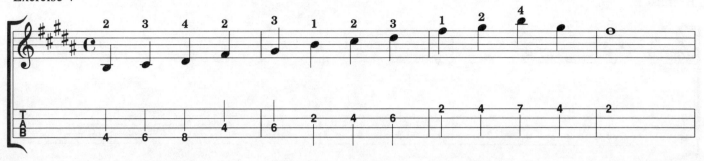

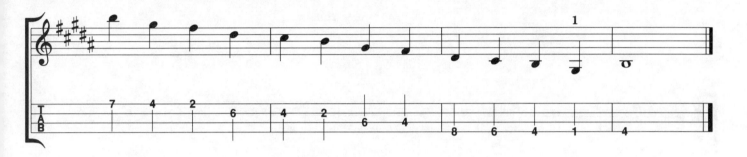

Ab Pentatonic Scale

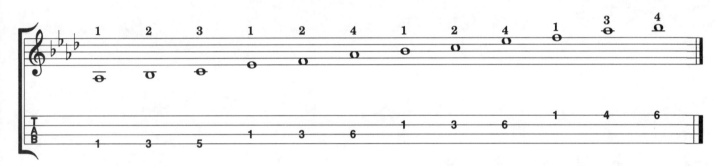

Exercise 1

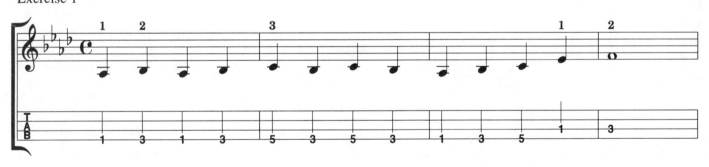

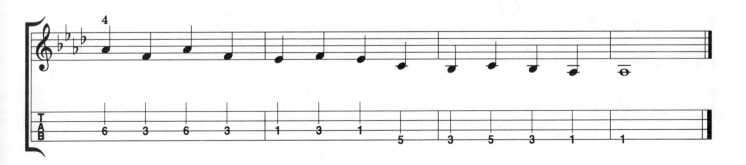

Exercise 2

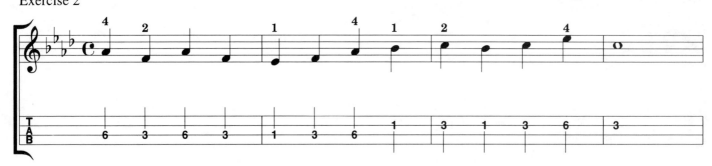

Exercise 3

Exercise 4

F♯ Pentatonic Scale

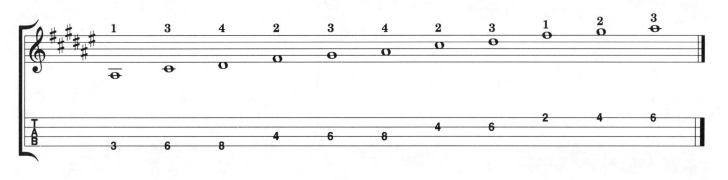

Exercise 1

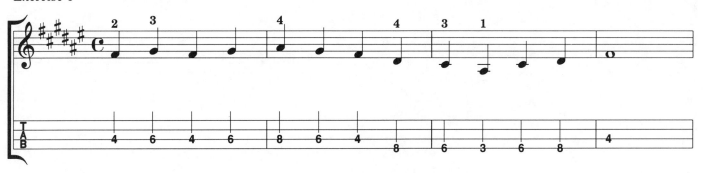

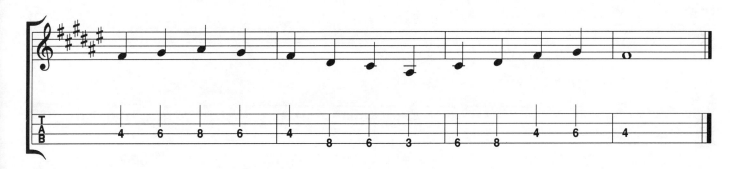

25

Exercise 2

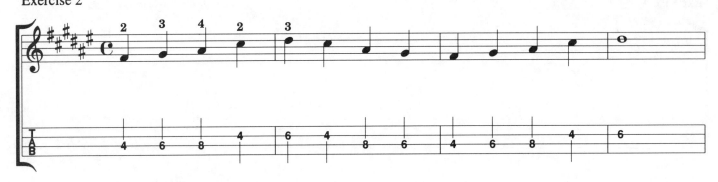

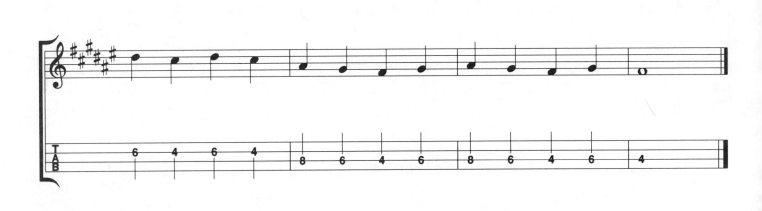

Exercise 3

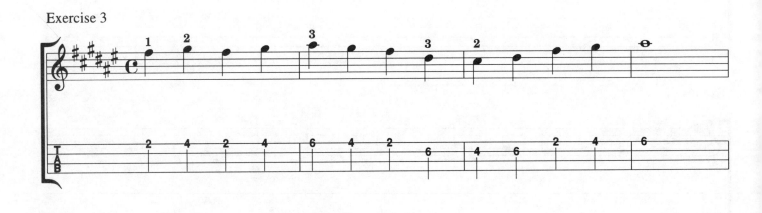

26

Exercise 4

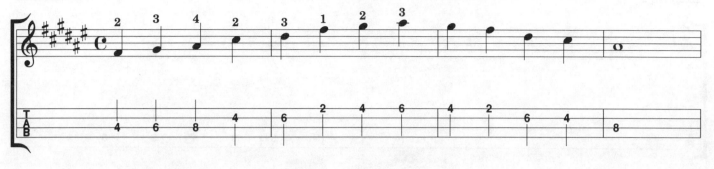

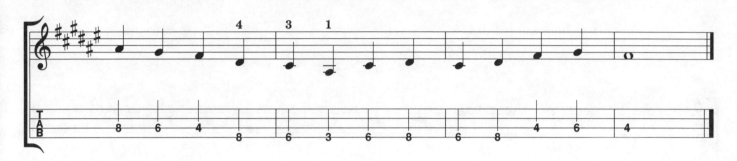

Db Pentatonic Scale

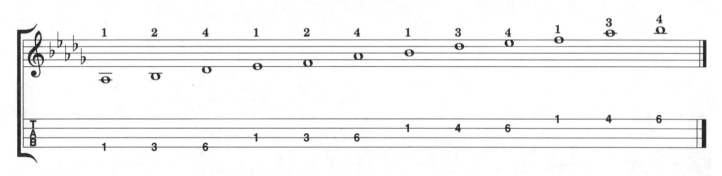

Exercise 1

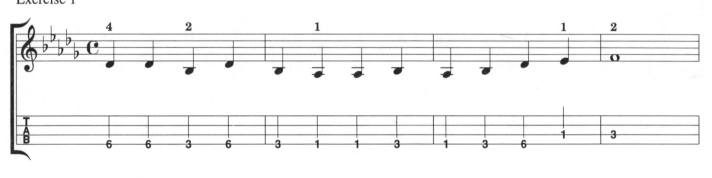

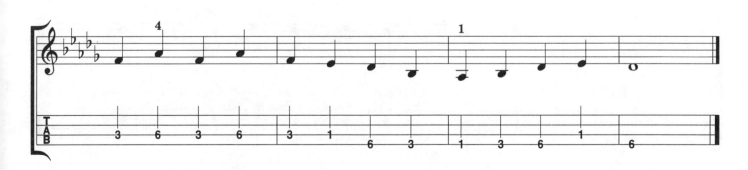

Exercise 2

Exercise 3

Exercise 4

C♯ Pentatonic Scale

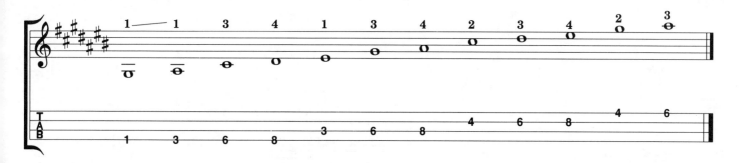

Exercise 1

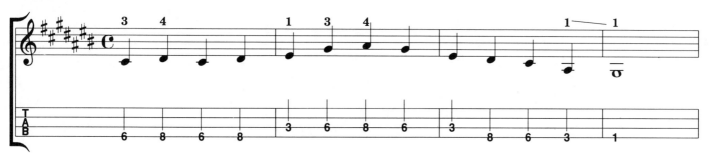

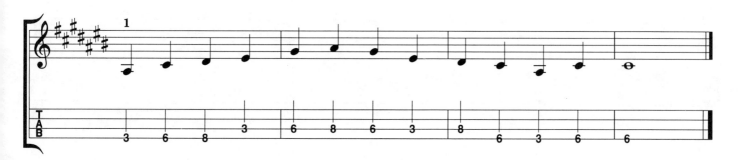

Exercise 2

Exercise 3

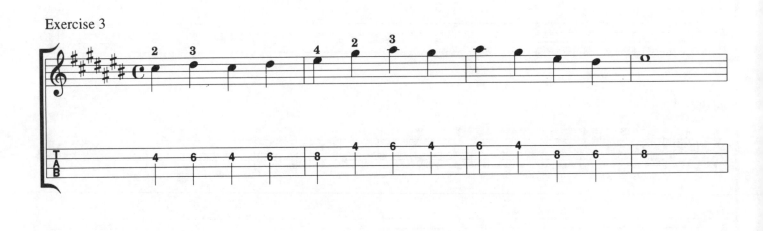

Exercise 4

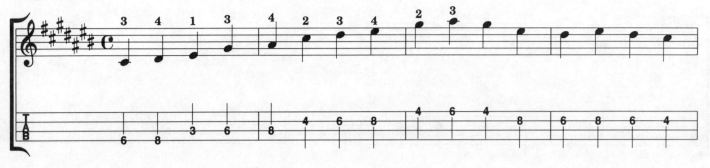

G♭ Pentatonic Scale

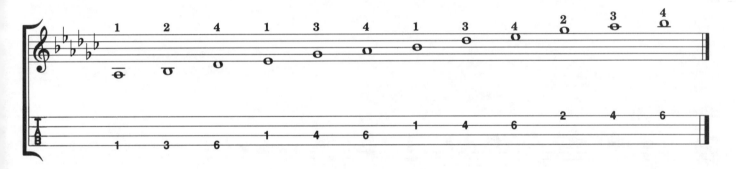

Exercise 1

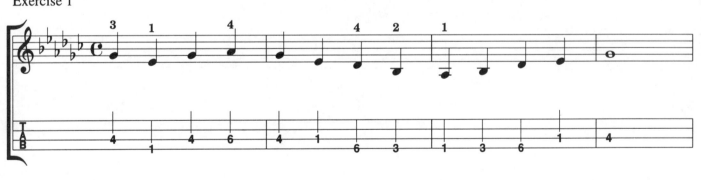

Exercise 2

Exercise 3

Exercise 4

Cb Pentatonic Scale

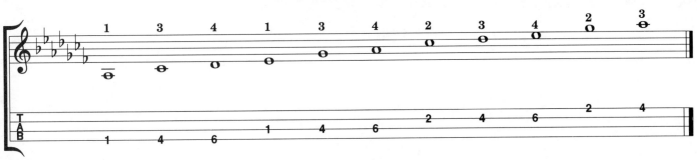

Exercise 1

Exercise 2

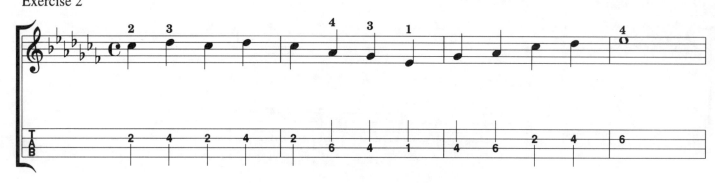

Exercise 3

Exercise 4

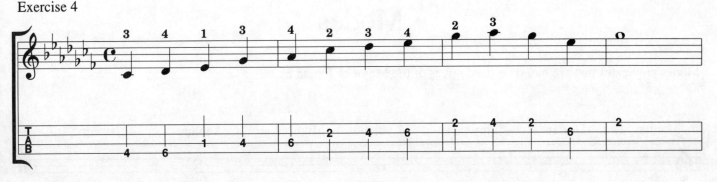

35

Modes

Modes are Scales that are based on the degrees of the Major or Ionian Scale.

Ionian   Dorian   Phrygian   Lydian   Mixolydian   Aeolian   Locrian

Ionian

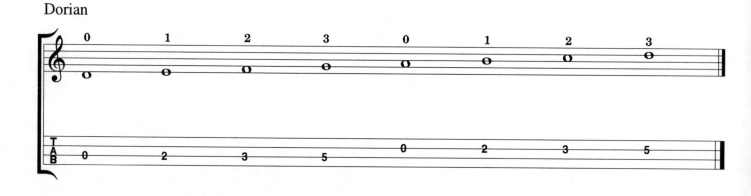

Dorian

Phrygian

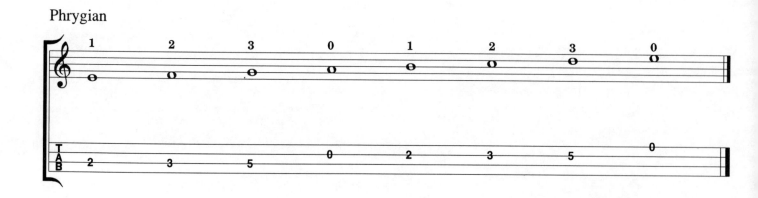

Lydian

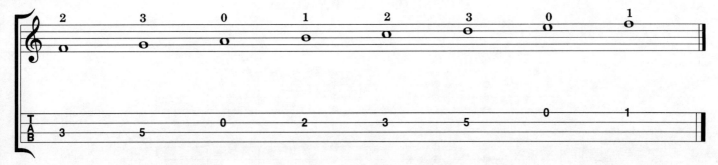

Mixolydian

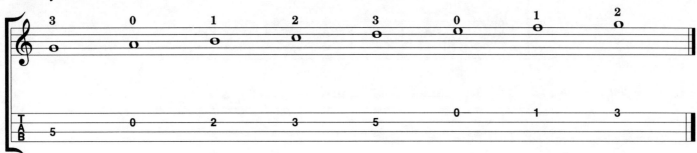

Aeolian

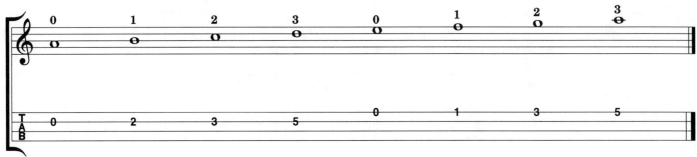

Locrian

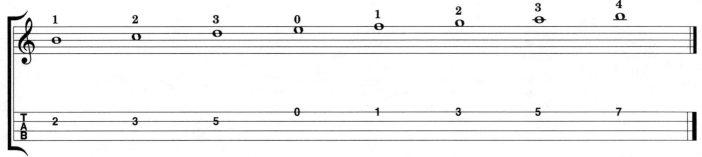

I Position Major Scales

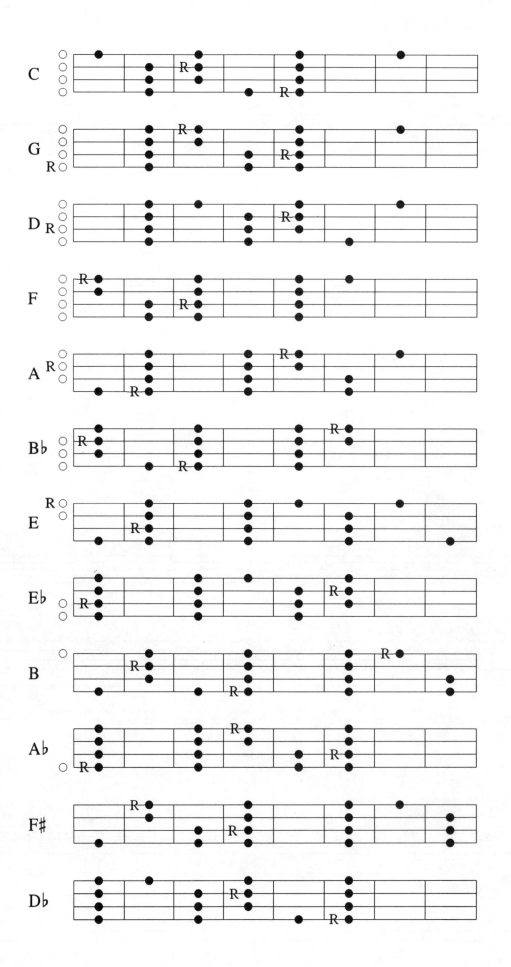

C Major Scale

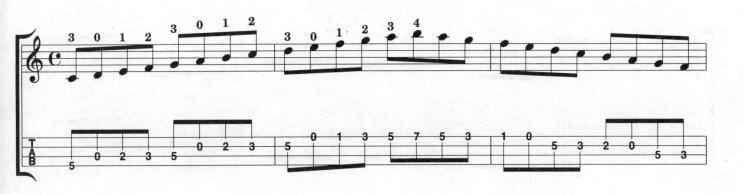

G Major Scale

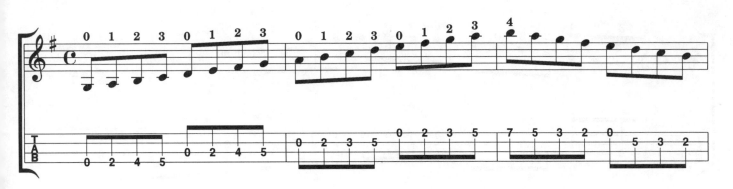

D Major Scale

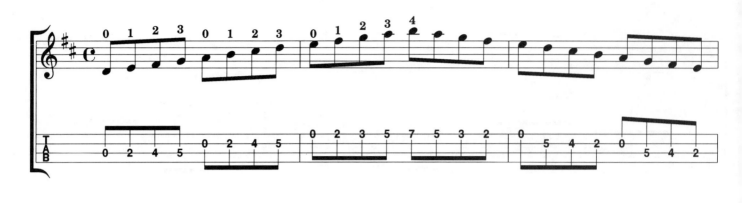

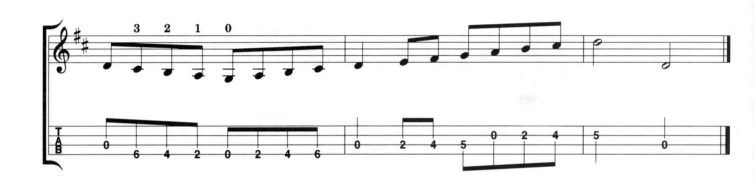

F Major Scale

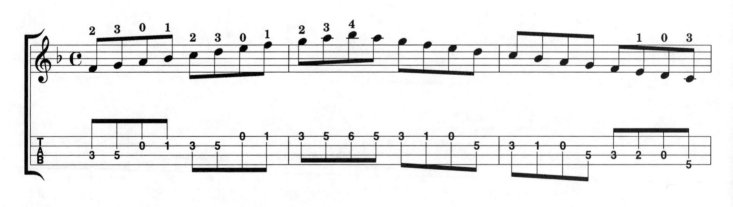

A Major Scale

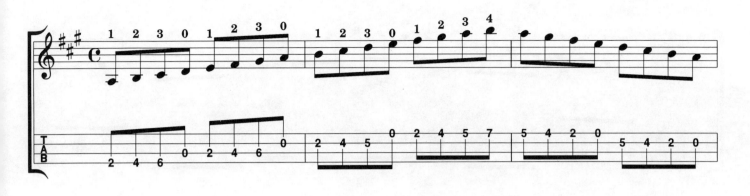

B♭ Major Scale

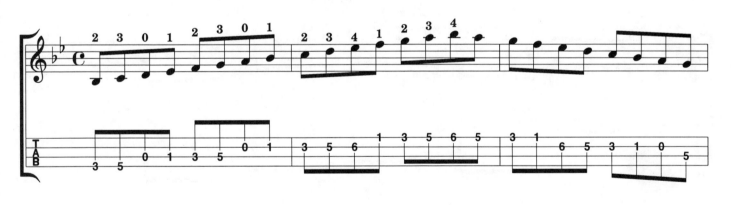

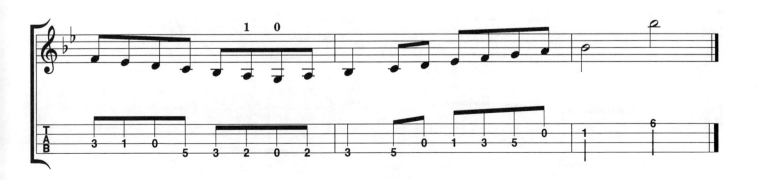

E Major Scale

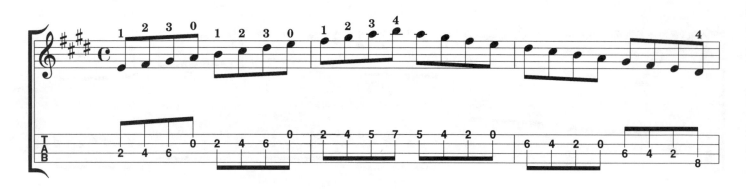

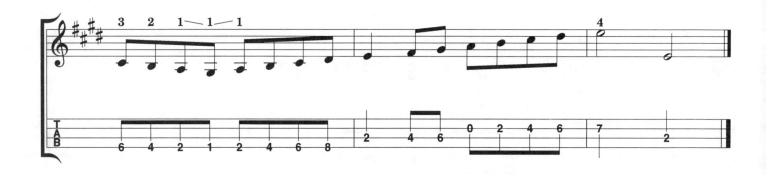

E♭ Major Scale

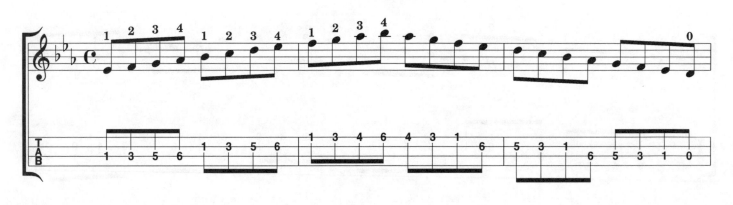

B Major Scale

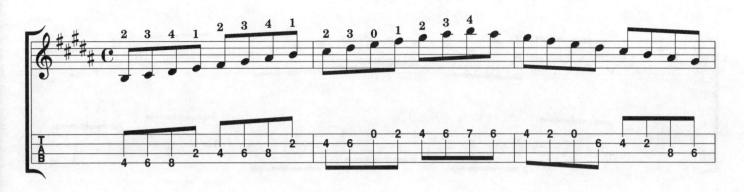

A♭ Major Scale

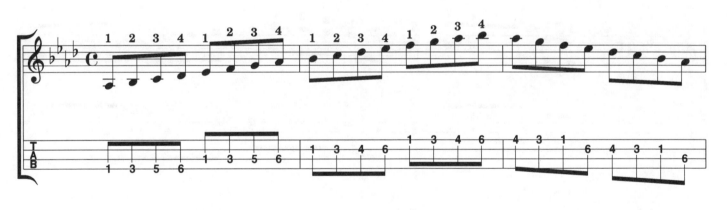

F# Major Scale

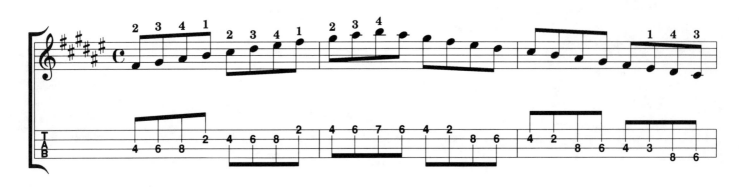

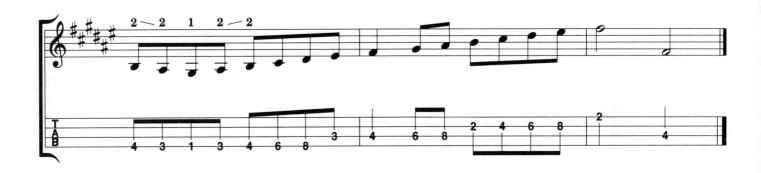

Db Major Scale

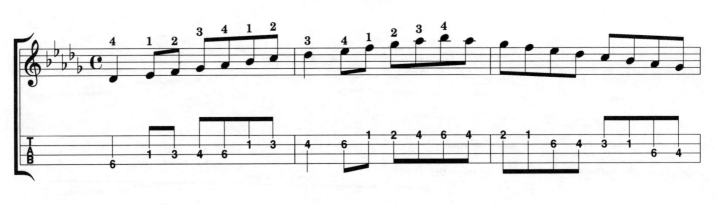

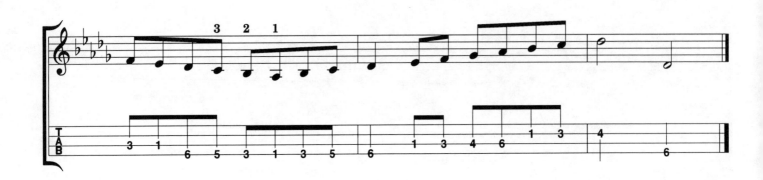

C♯ Major Scale

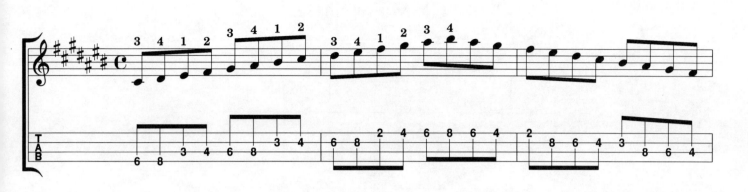

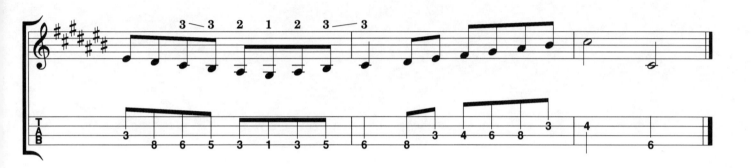

G♭ Major Scale

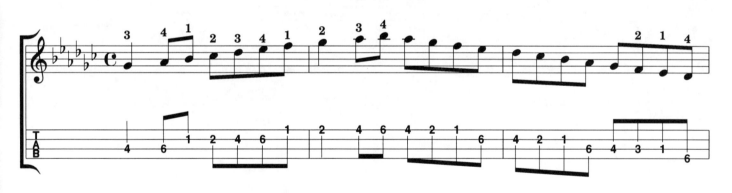

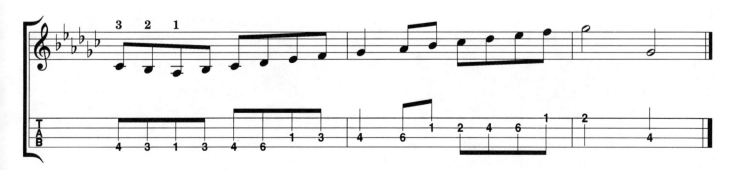

Fingering Pattern For
C♭ Major Scale

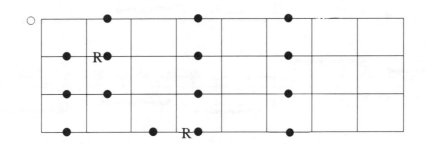

C♭ Major Scale

Minor Scales

The minor scales are based on the sixth degree of the majors.
In this book there are three forms of minor scales; Pure, Harmonic, and Melodic.
In the Pure Minor Scale, there are no altered notes to the key.
The Harmonic Minor Scale has the seventh tone raised one half step.
The Melodic Minor Scale has the sixth and seventh tones raised one half step ascending, but are returned to notes natural to the key on the descent.

I Position Minor Scales

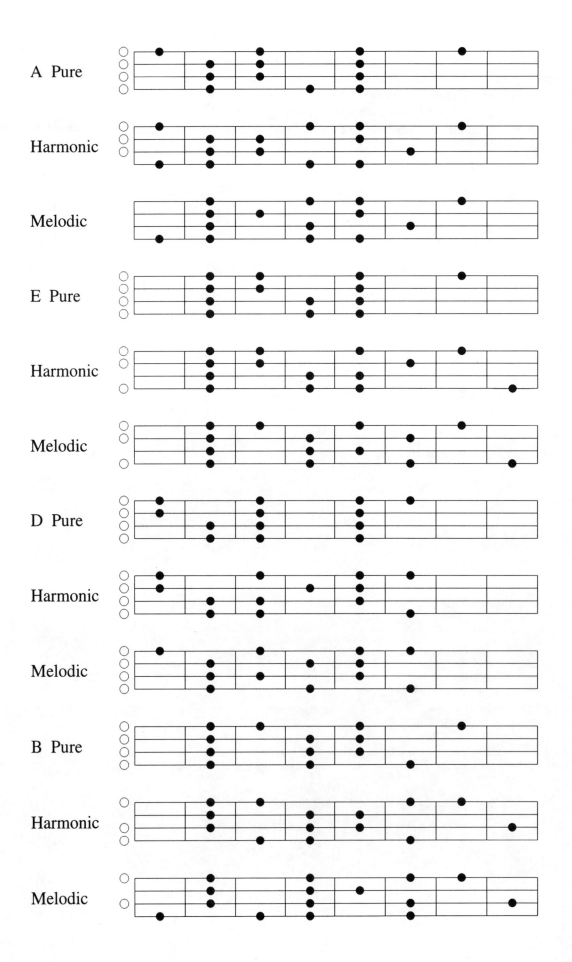

A Pure Minor Scale

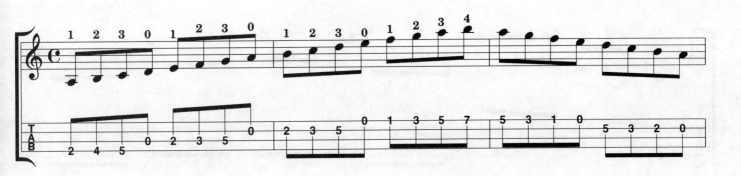

A Harmonic Minor Scale

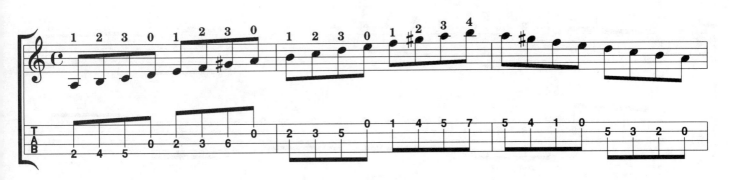

A Melodic Minor Scale

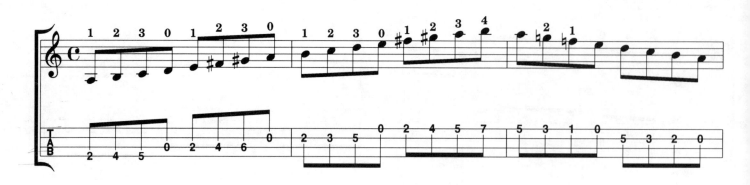

E Pure Minor Scale

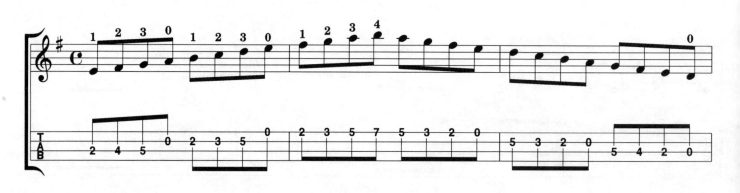

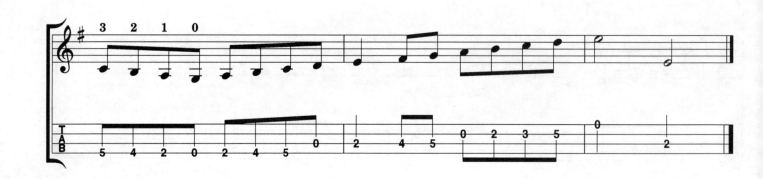

E Harmonic Minor Scale

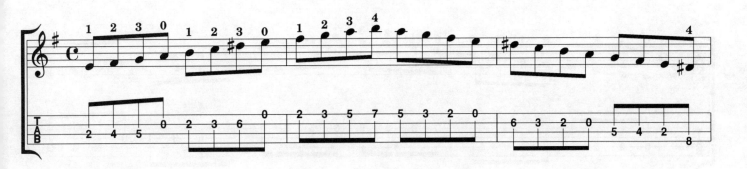

E Melodic Minor Scale

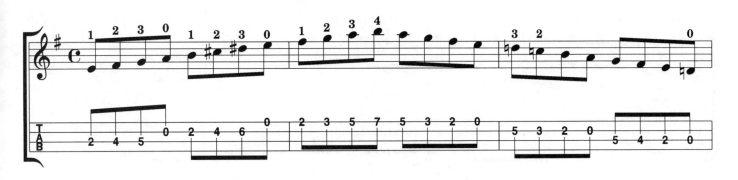

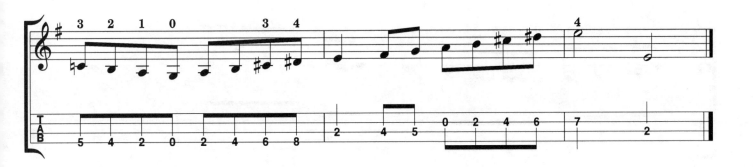

D Pure Minor Scale

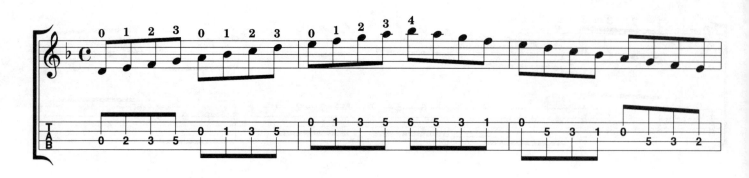

D Harmonic Minor Scale

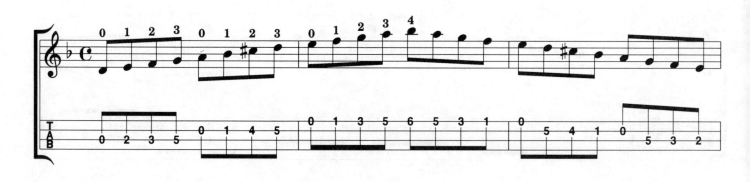

D Melodic Minor Scale

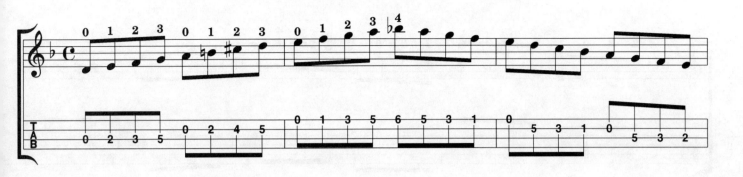

B Pure Minor Scale

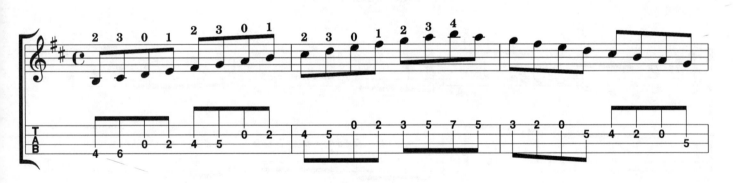

B Harmonic Minor Scale

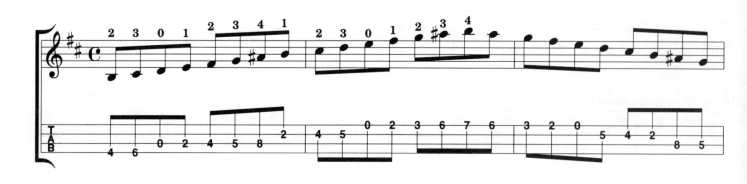

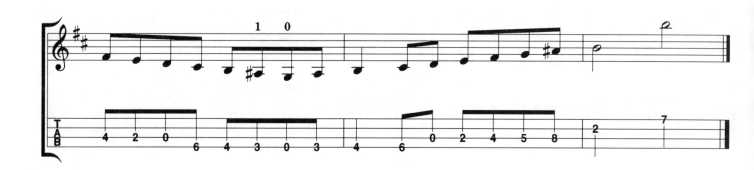

B Melodic Minor Scale

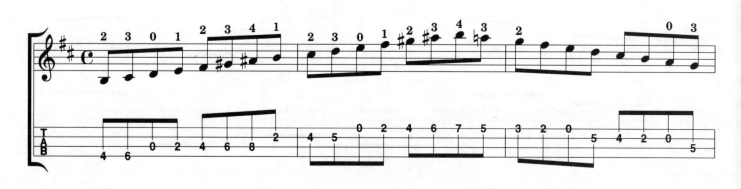

I Position Minor Scales

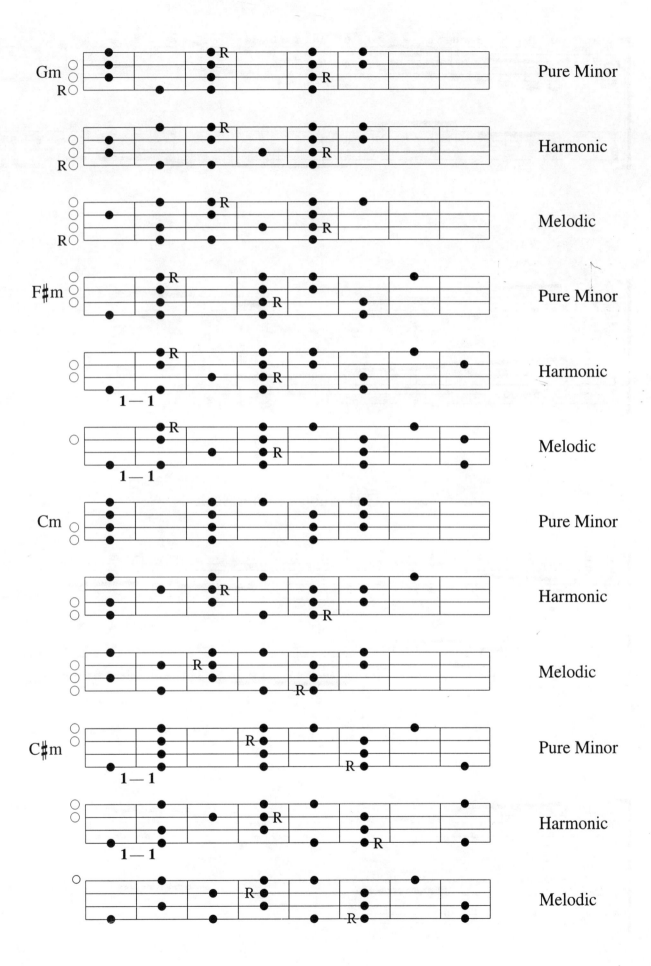

G Pure Minor Scale

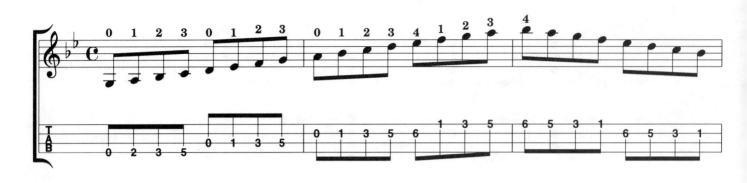

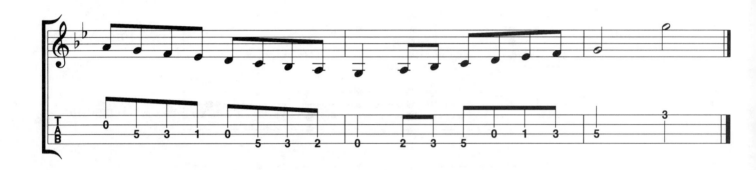

G Harmonic Minor Scale

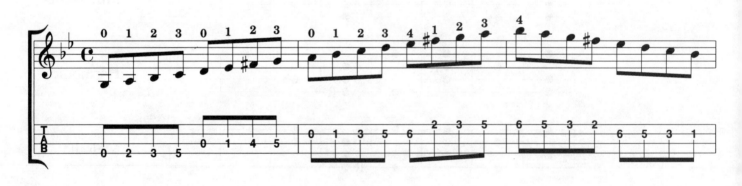

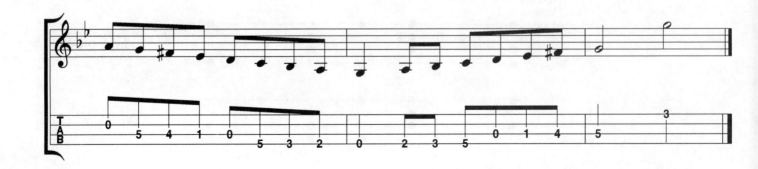

G Melodic Minor Scale

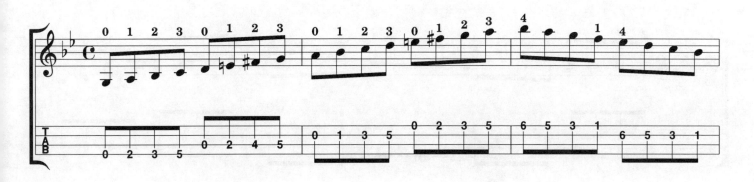

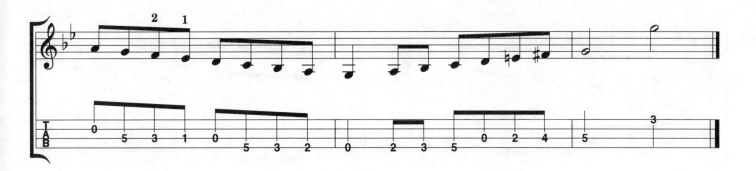

F# Pure Minor Scale

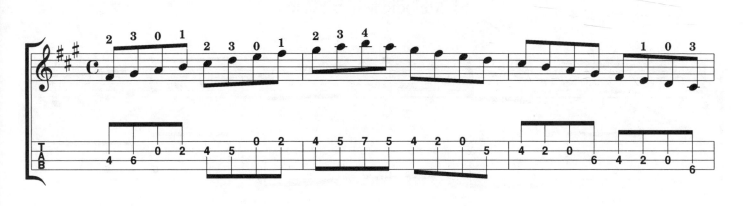

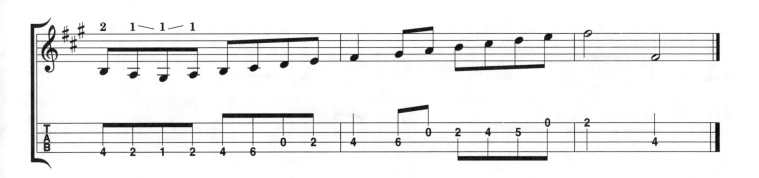

F♯ Harmonic Minor Scale

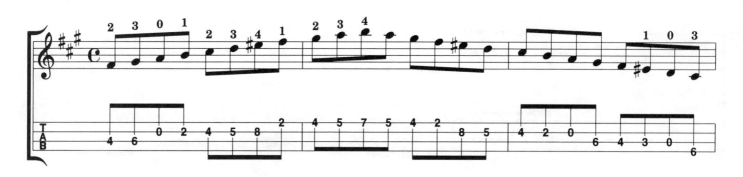

F♯ Melodic Minor Scale

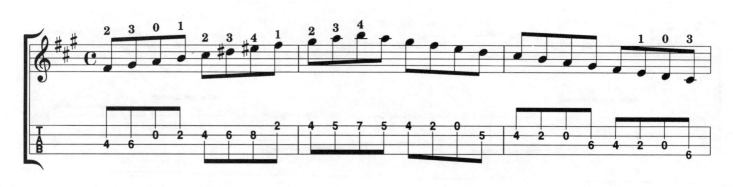

C Pure Minor Scale

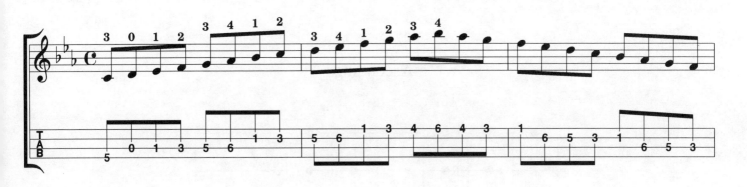

C Harmonic Minor Scale

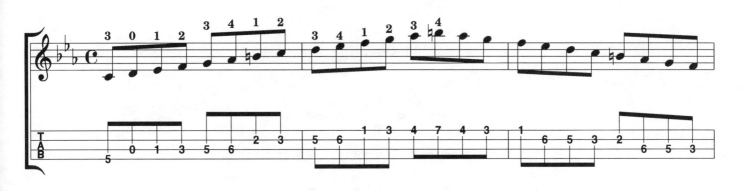

59

In the C Melodic Minor Scale the A and B are used to resolve to C, but in first position the highest note is B, so to avoid odd intervals in the second measure the A and B will remain flat.

Ascending

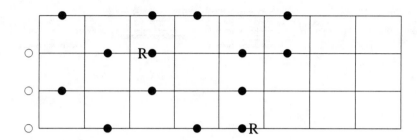

Descending

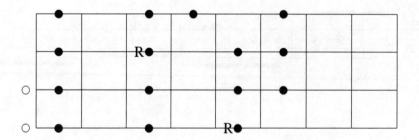

C Melodic Minor Scale

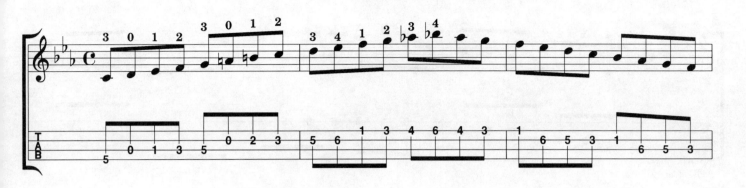

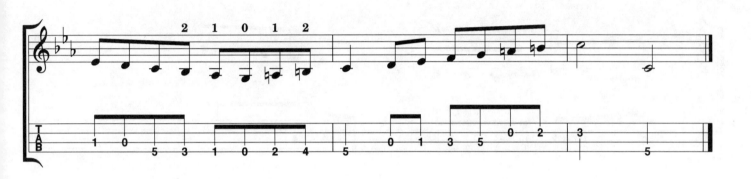

C# Pure Minor Scale

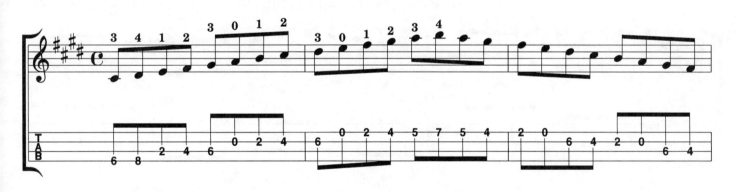

C# Harmonic Minor Scale

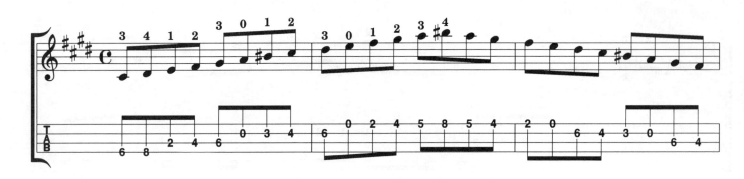

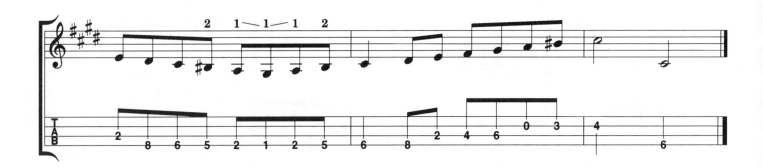

C# Melodic Minor Scale

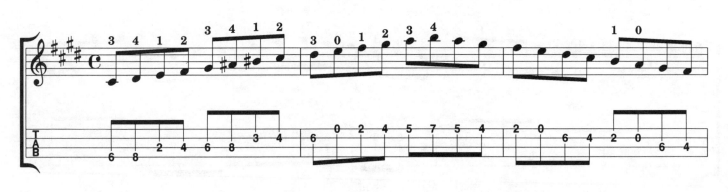

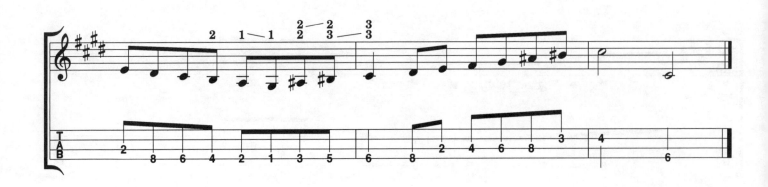

I Position Minor Scales

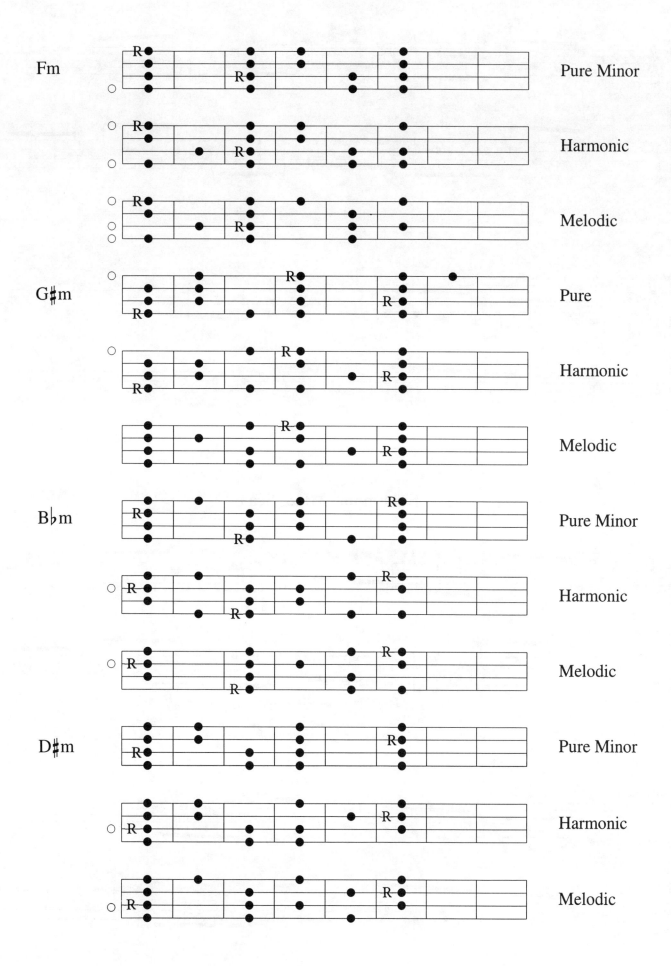

F Pure Minor Scale

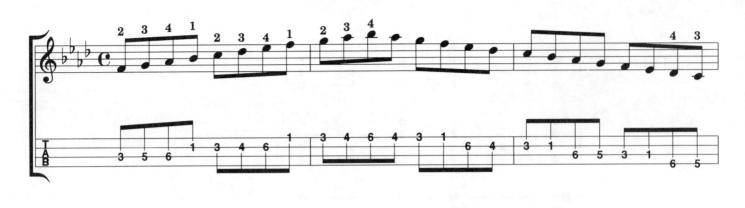

F Harmonic Minor Scale

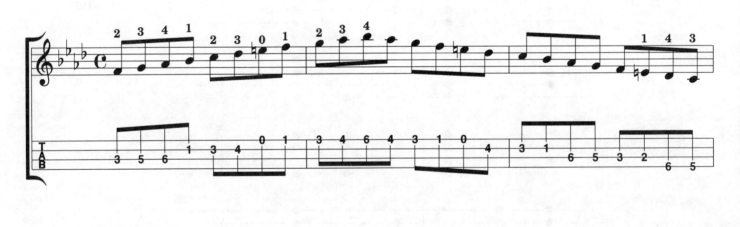

F Melodic Minor Scale

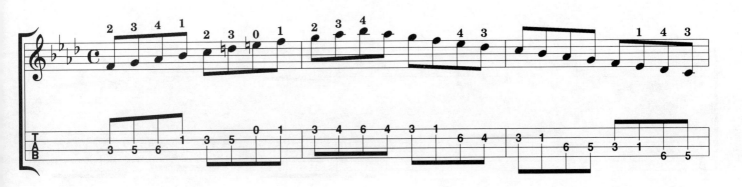

G# Pure Minor Scale

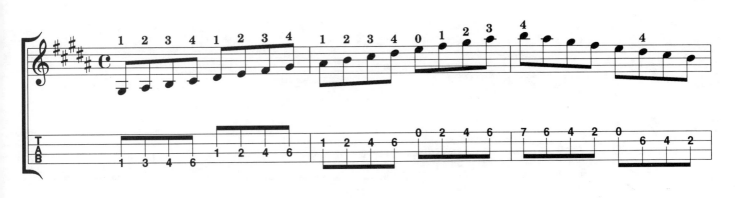

G♯ Harmonic Minor Scale

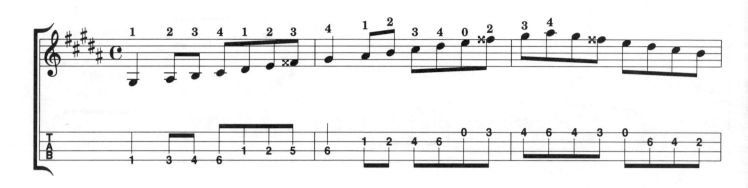

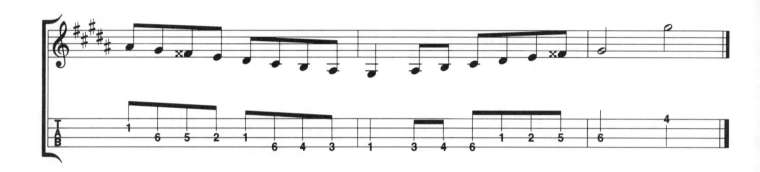

G♯ Melodic Minor Scale

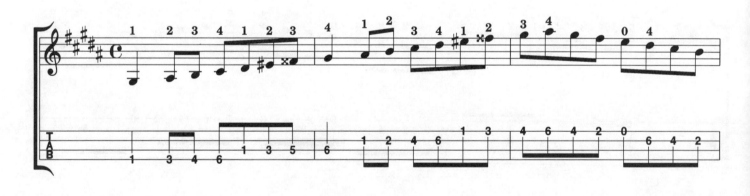

Another I Position Fingering for G♯ Minor

Pure Minor

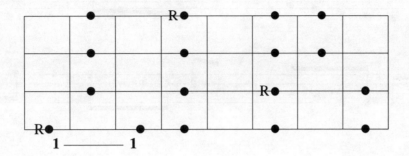

Harmonic Minor

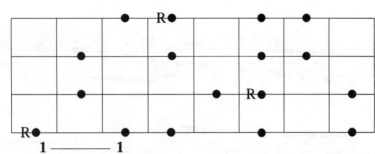

G♯ Pure Minor Scale

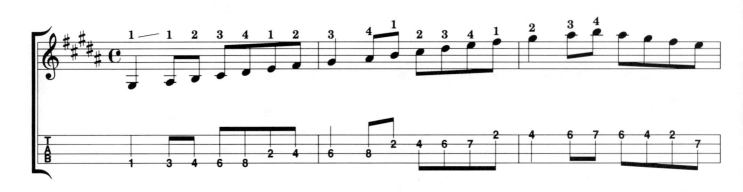

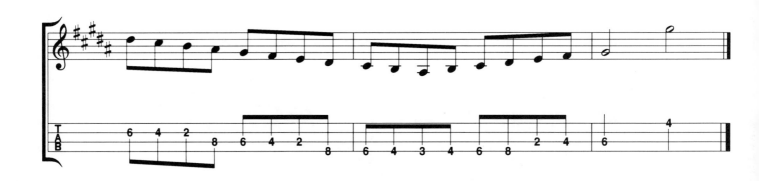

G♯ Harmonic Minor Scale

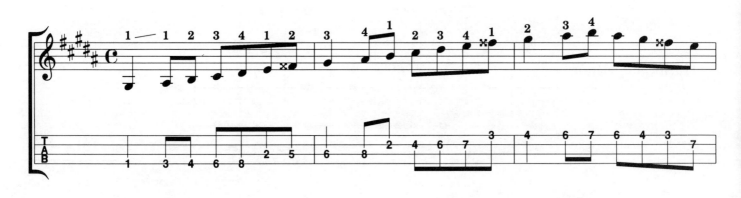

G♯ Melodic Minor Scale Ascending Pattern

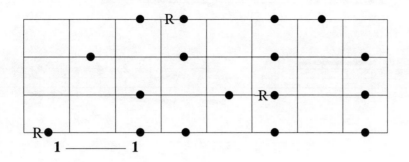

G♯ Melodic Minor Scale

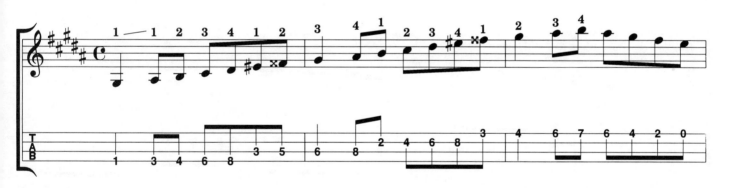

B♭ Pure Minor Scale

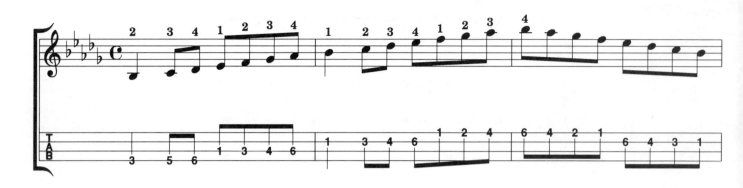

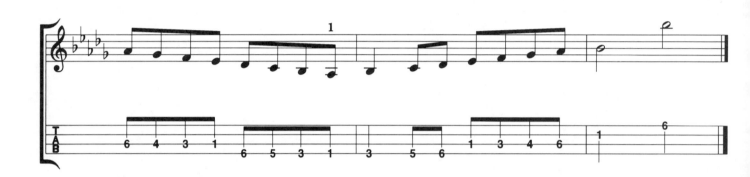

B♭ Harmonic Minor Scale

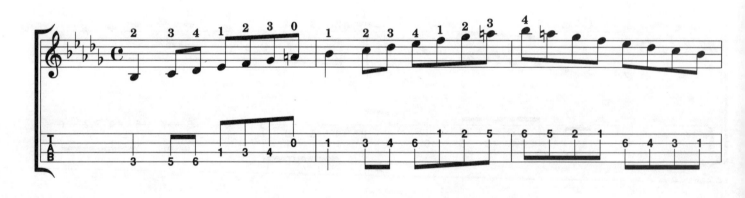

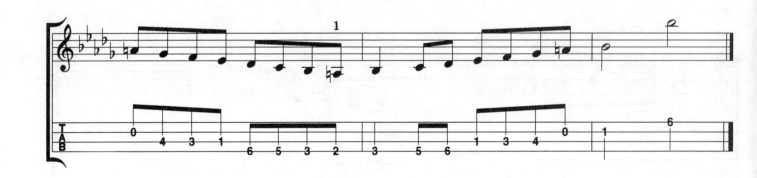

Bb Melodic Minor Scale

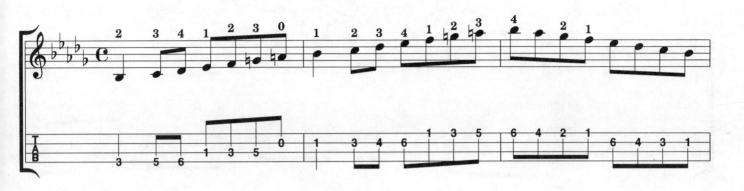

D# Pure Minor Scale

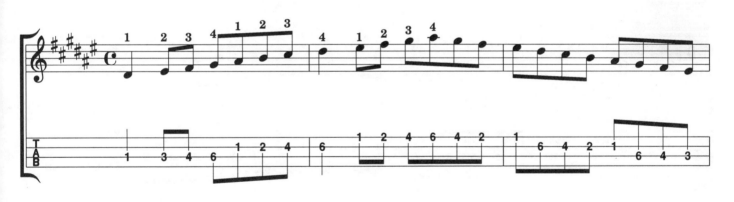

D♯ Harmonic Minor Scale

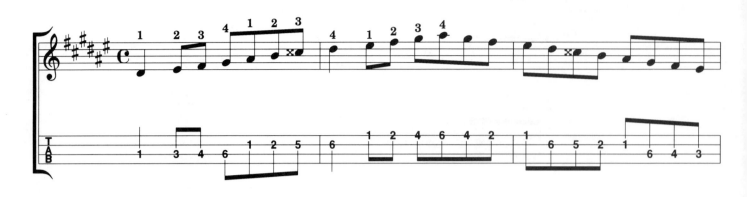

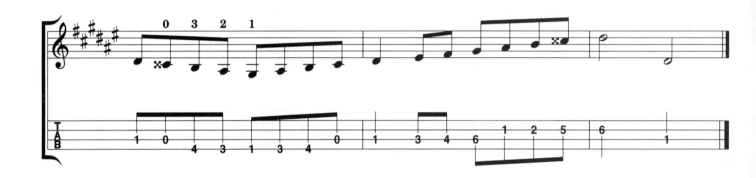

D♯ Melodic Minor Scale

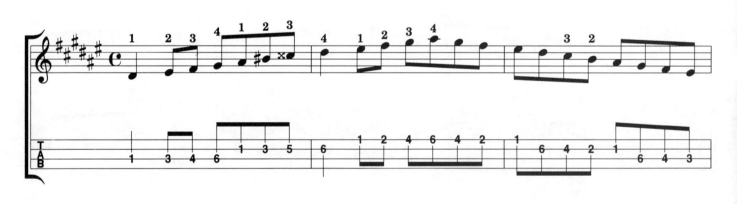

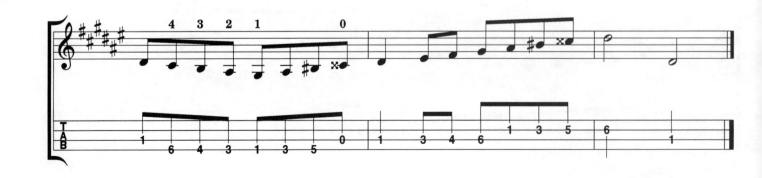

Another I Position Fingering for D♯ Minor

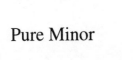

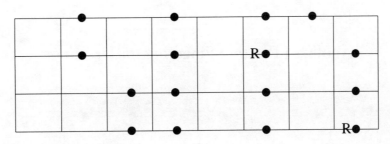

D♯ Pure Minor Scale

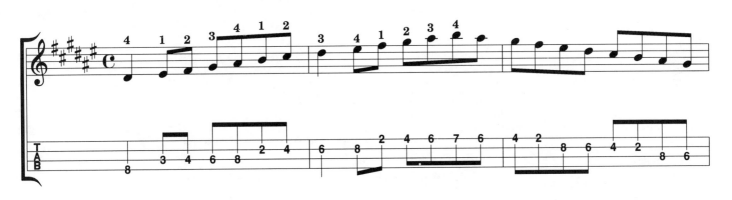

Another I Position Fingering for D♯ Minor

Harmonic

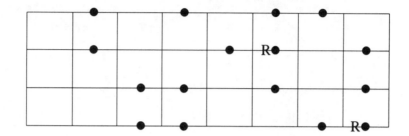

Melodic

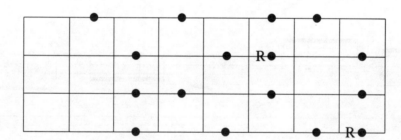

D♯ Harmonic Minor Scale

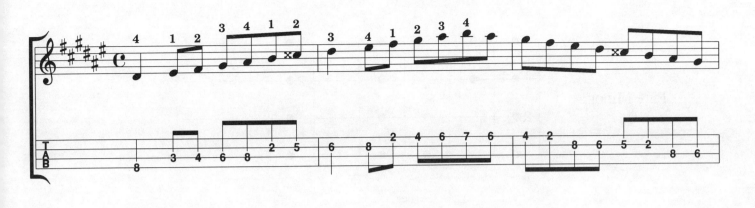

D♯ Melodic Minor Scale

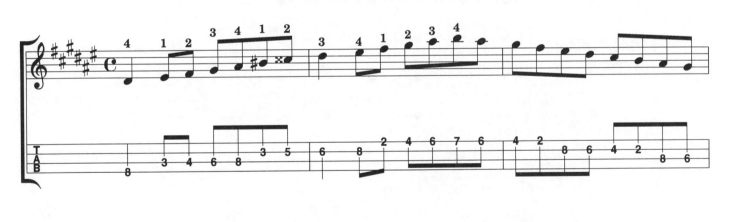

E♭ Minor Scales

Pure Minor

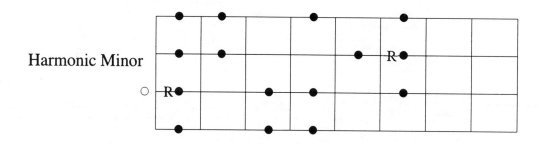

Harmonic Minor

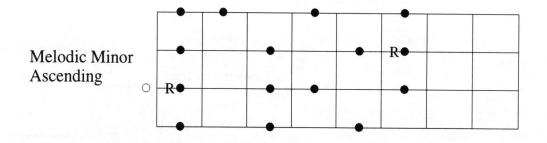

Melodic Minor
Ascending

E♭ Pure Minor Scale

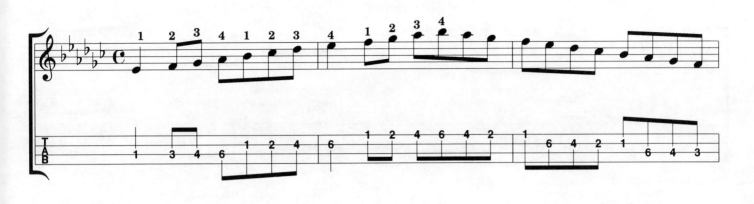

E♭ Harmonic Minor Scale

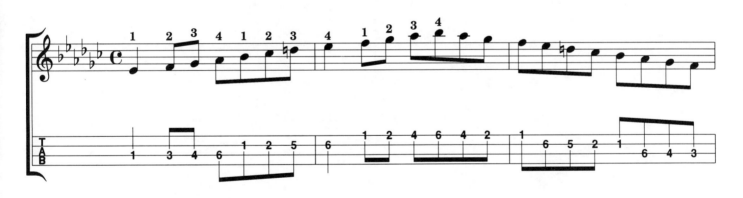

E♭ Melodic Minor Scale

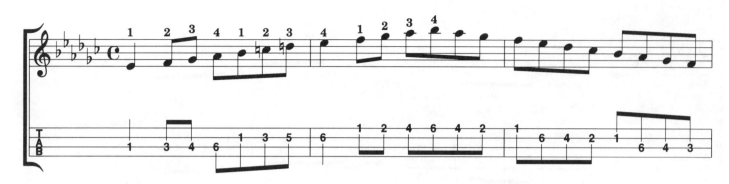

A♭ Minor Scales

Pure

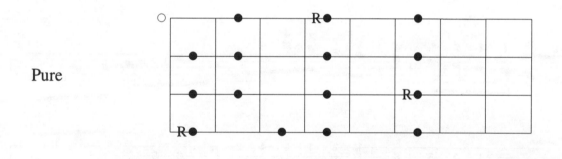

Harmonic

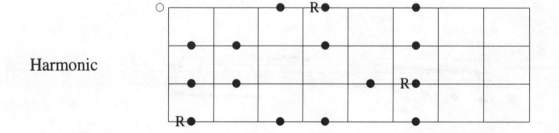

Ab Pure Minor Scale

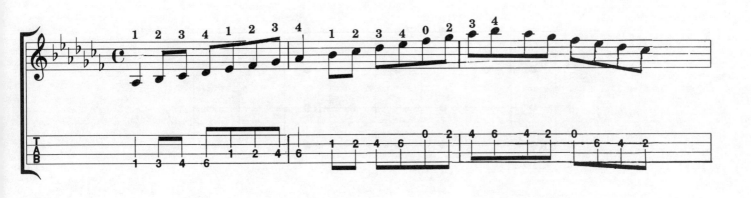

Ab Harmonic Minor Scale

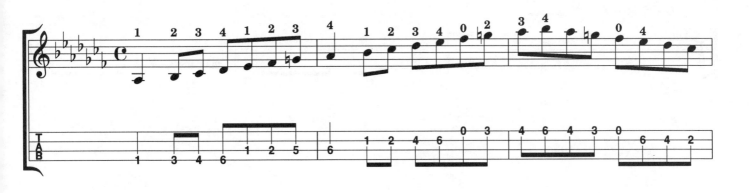

A♭ Melodic Minor Scale

Ascending only

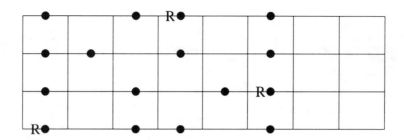

A♭ Melodic Minor Scale

I Position C Chromatic Scale

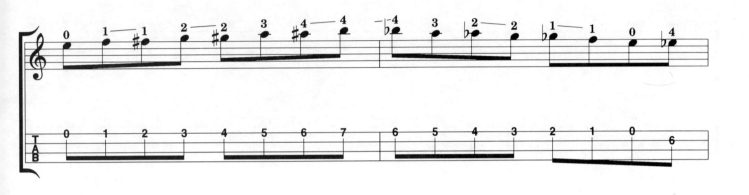

C Diminished Scale

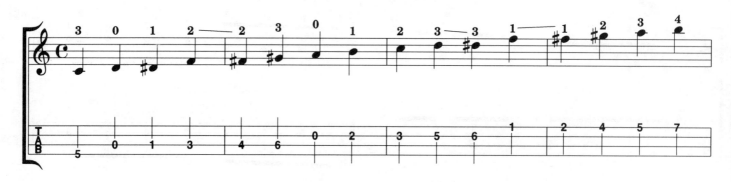

C# Diminished Scale

D Diminished Scale

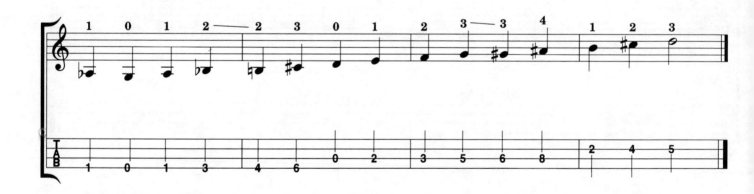

Positions

Positions are determined by the fret in which the first finger is placed.
Fingers are assigned to certain notes and when sharps or flats occur they will move up or down one fret.

Example

II Position

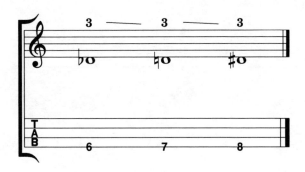

I Position

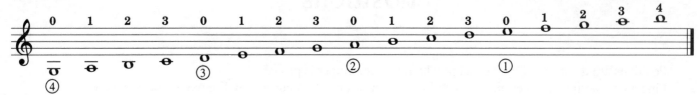

II Position

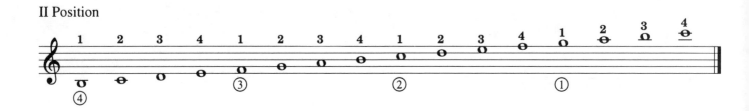

III Position

IV

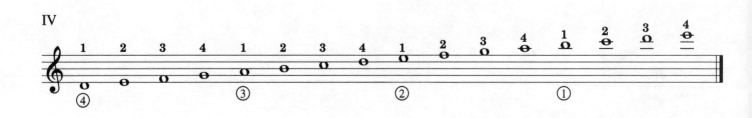

V

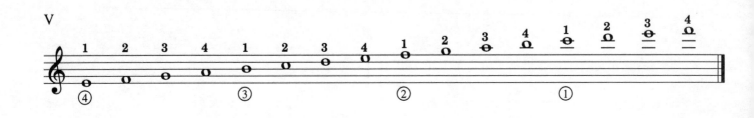

II Position Major Scales

All diagrams begin at the 3rd fret.

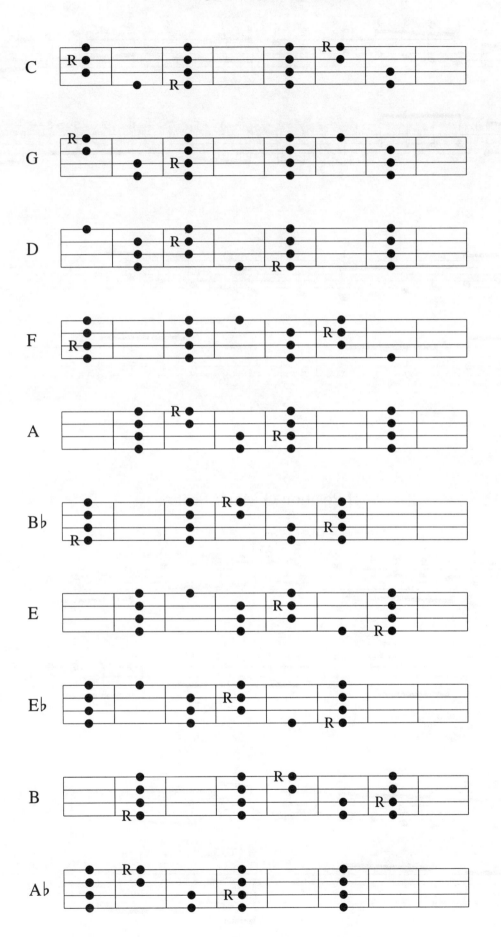

II Position C Major Scale

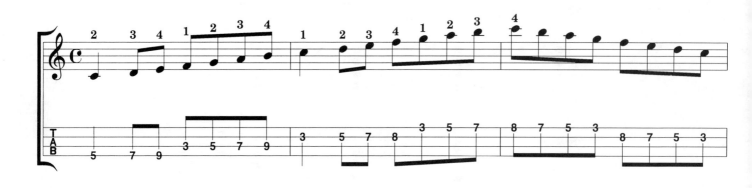

II Position G Major Scale

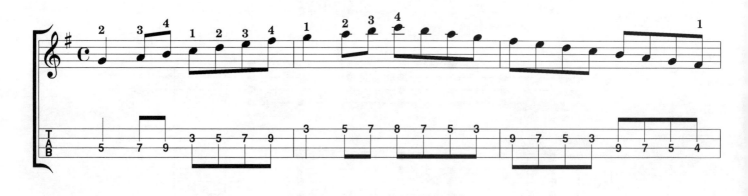

II Position D Major Scale

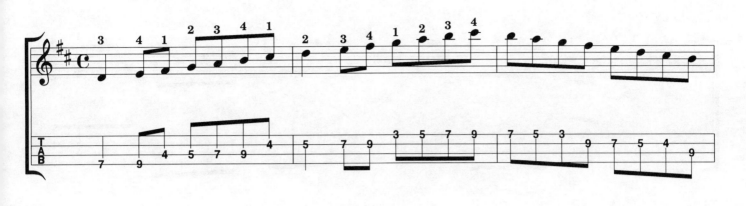

II Position F Major Scale

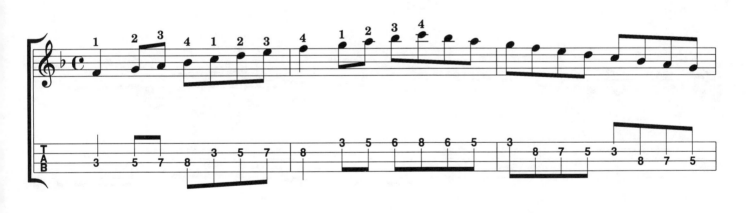

II Position A Major Scale

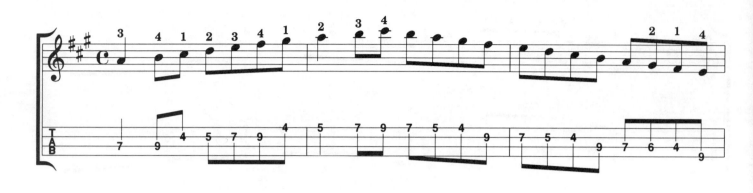

II Position B♭ Major Scale

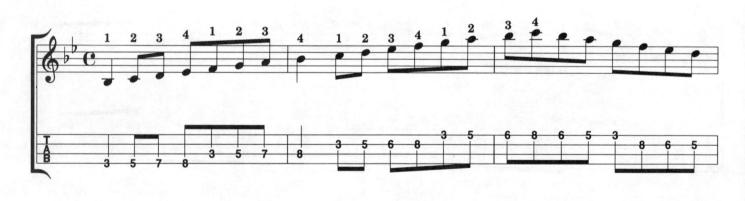

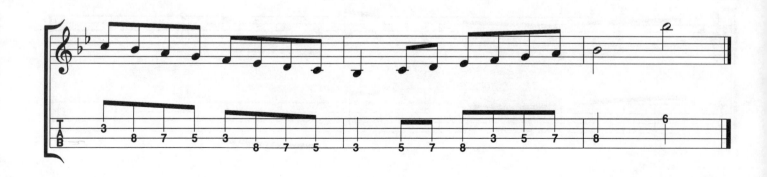

II Position E Major Scale

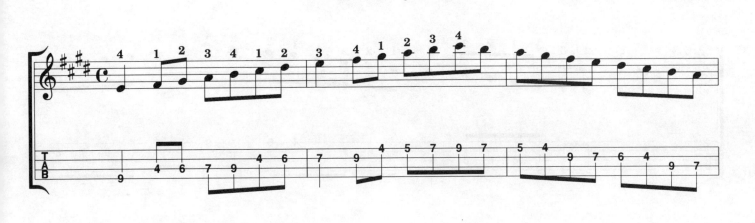

II Position E♭ Major Scale

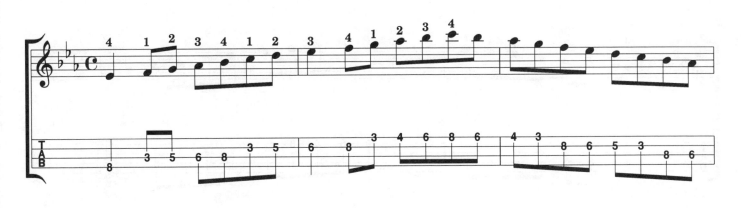

91

II Position B Major Scale

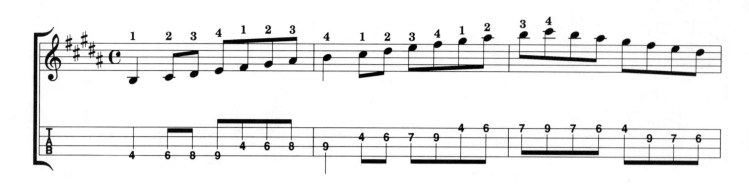

II Position A♭ Major Scale

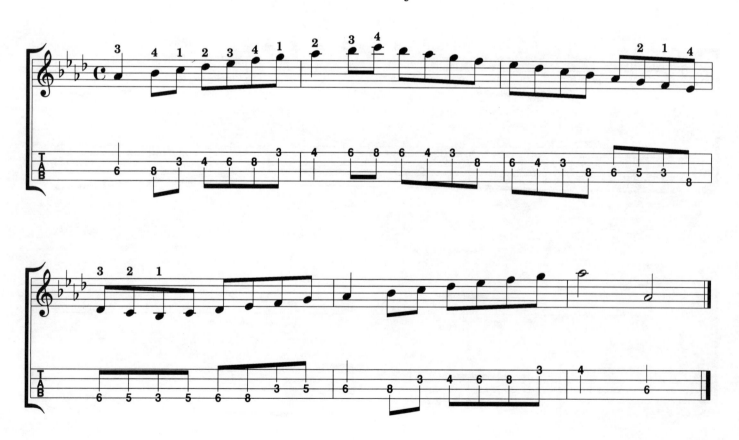

II Position F♯ Major Scale

Diagram starts on the 4th fret.

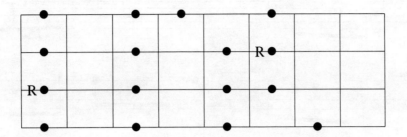

II Position D♭ Major Scale

Diagram starts on the 2nd fret.

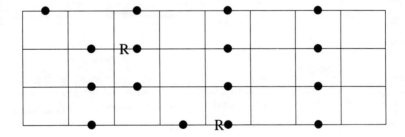

II Position F# Major Scale

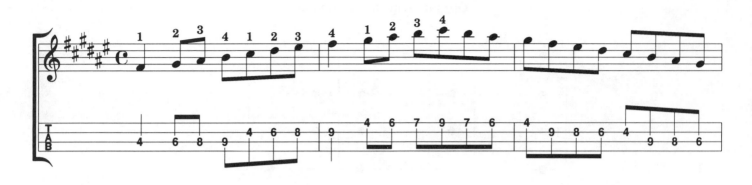

II Position Db Major Scale

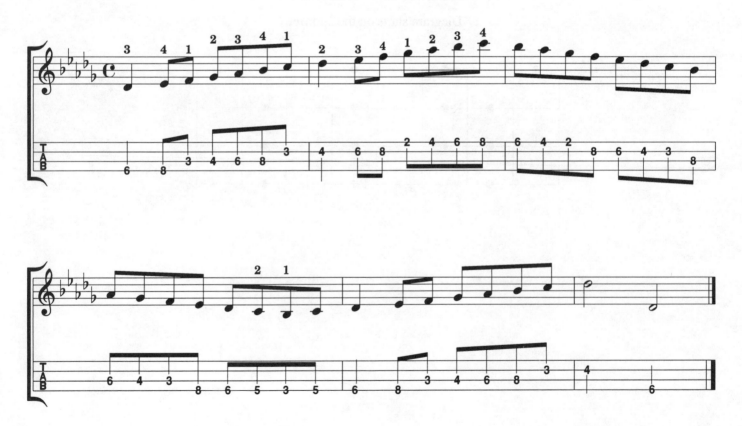

II Position C♯ Major Scale

Diagram begins at the 4th fret.

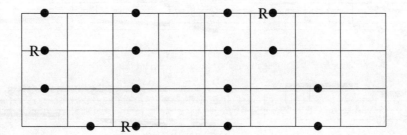

II Position G♭ Major Scale

Diagram begins at the 2nd fret.

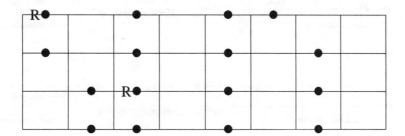

II Position C♯ Major Scale

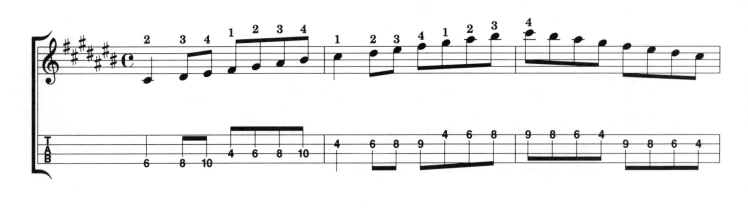

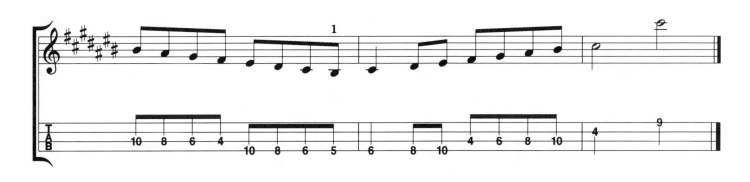

II Position G♭ Major Scale

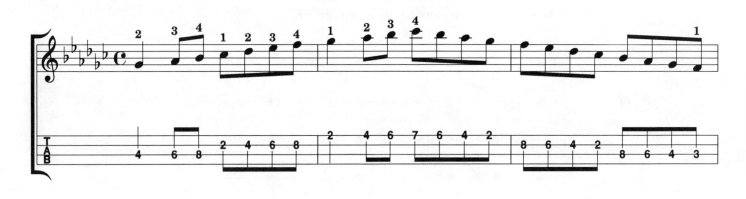

Fingering Pattern for
II Position C♭ Major Scale

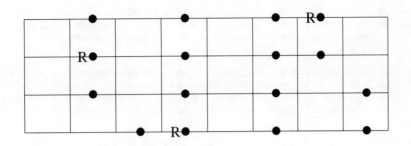

II Position C♭ Scale

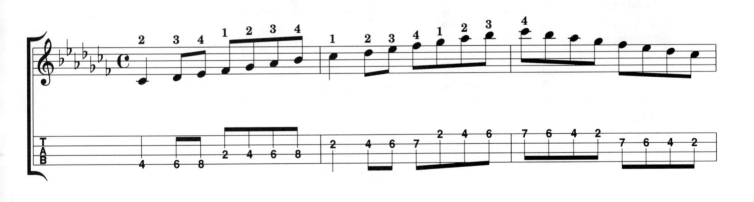

II Position Minor Scales
All diagrams start at the third fret.

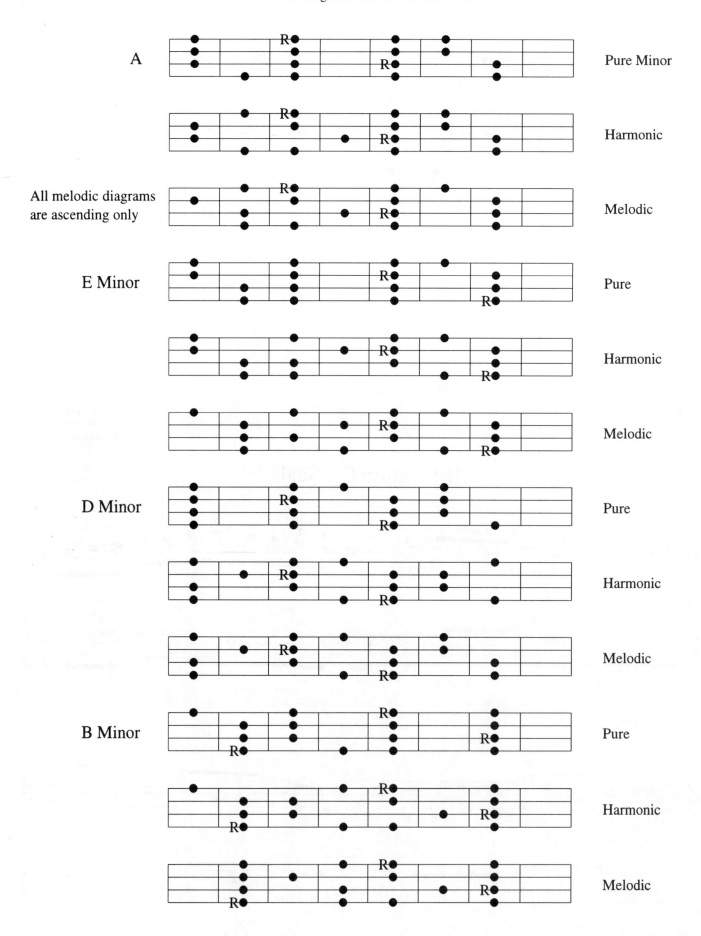

A — Pure Minor

Harmonic

All melodic diagrams are ascending only — Melodic

E Minor — Pure

Harmonic

Melodic

D Minor — Pure

Harmonic

Melodic

B Minor — Pure

Harmonic

Melodic

II Position A Pure Minor Scale

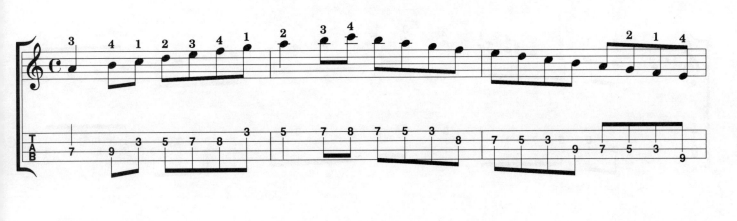

II Position A Harmonic Minor Scale

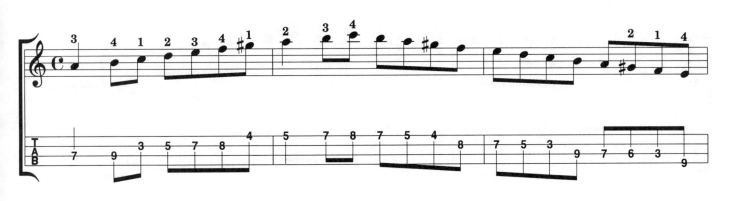

II Position A Melodic Minor Scale

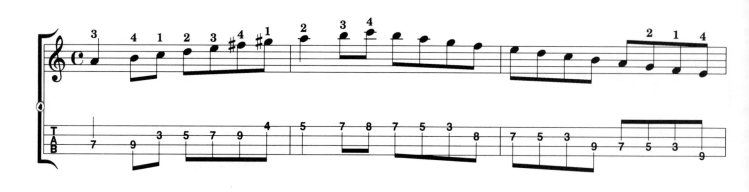

II Position E Pure Minor Scale

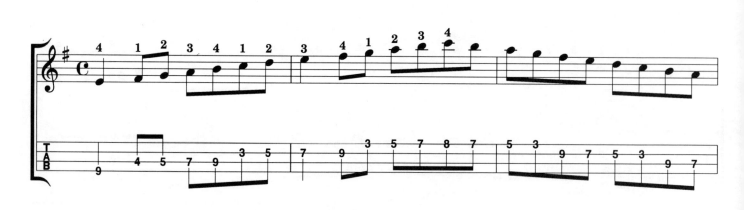

II Position E Harmonic Minor Scale

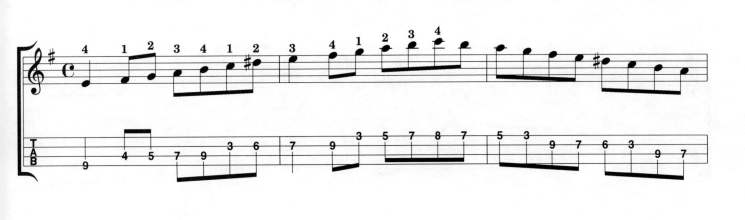

II Position E Melodic Minor Scale

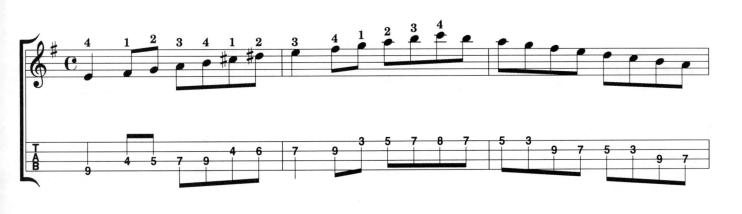

II Position D Pure Minor Scale

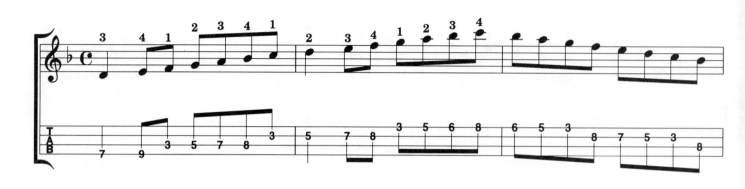

II Position D Harmonic Minor Scale

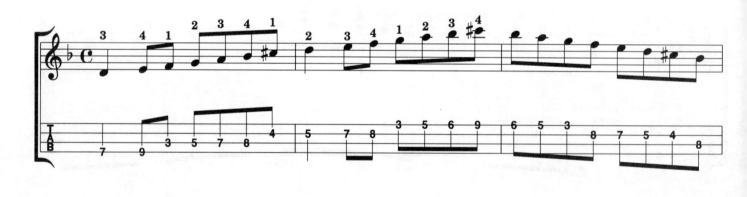

II Position D Melodic Minor Scale

II Position B Pure Minor Scale

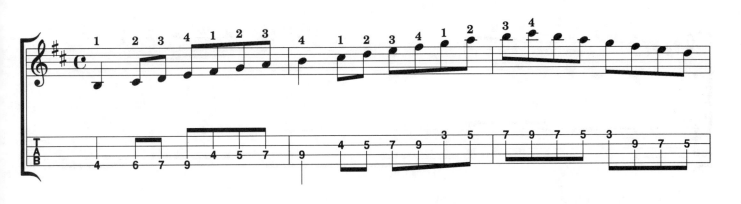

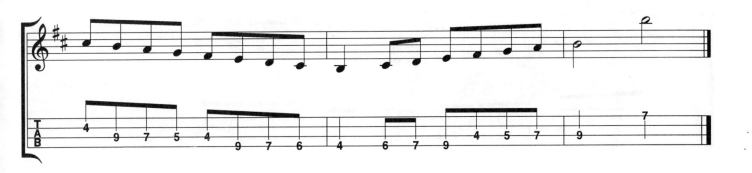

II Position B Harmonic Minor Scale

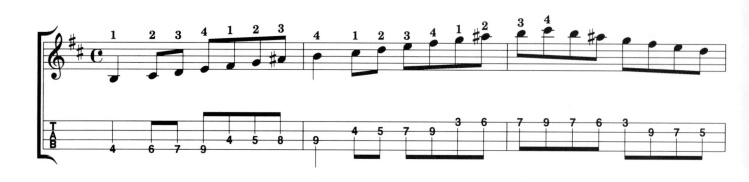

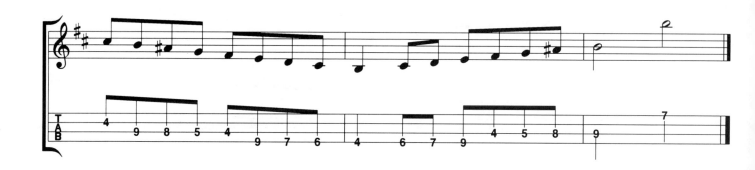

II Position B Melodic Minor Scale

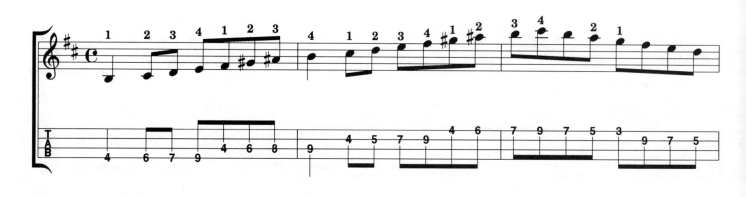

II Position Minor Scales
All diagrams start at the 3rd fret.

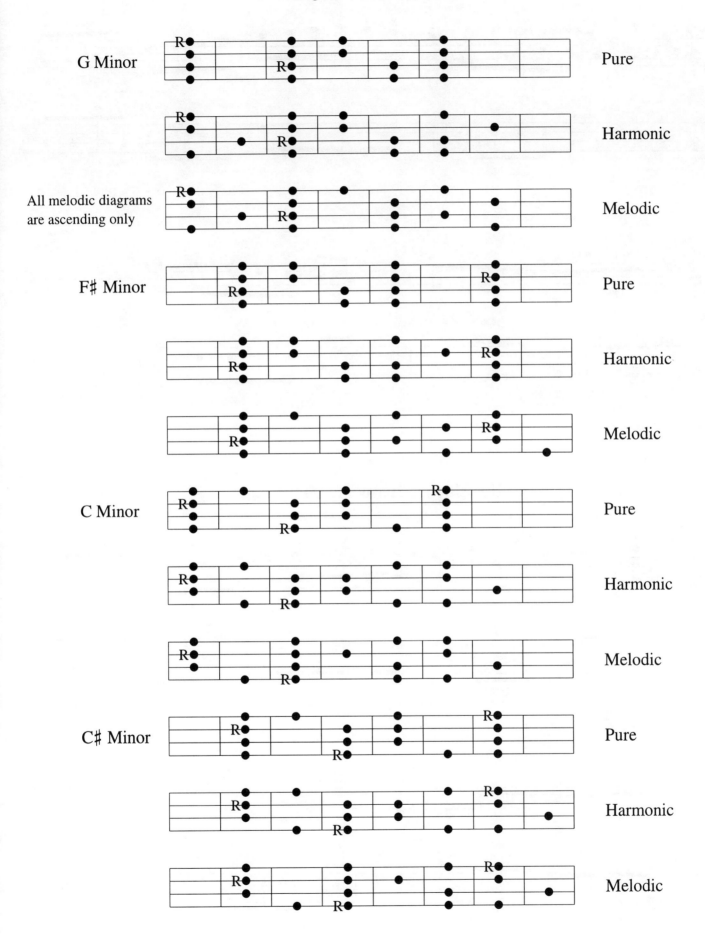

G Minor — Pure

G Minor — Harmonic

All melodic diagrams are ascending only — Melodic

F# Minor — Pure

F# Minor — Harmonic

F# Minor — Melodic

C Minor — Pure

C Minor — Harmonic

C Minor — Melodic

C# Minor — Pure

C# Minor — Harmonic

C# Minor — Melodic

II Position G Pure Minor Scale

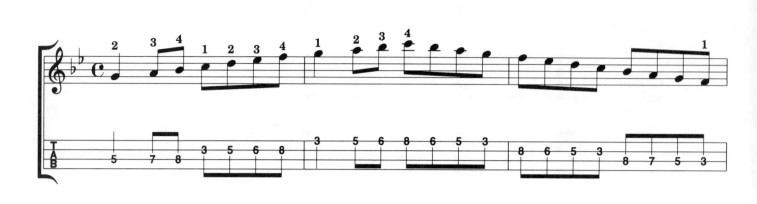

II Position G Harmonic Minor Scale

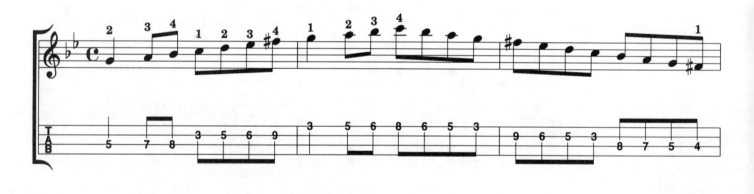

II Position G Melodic Minor Scale

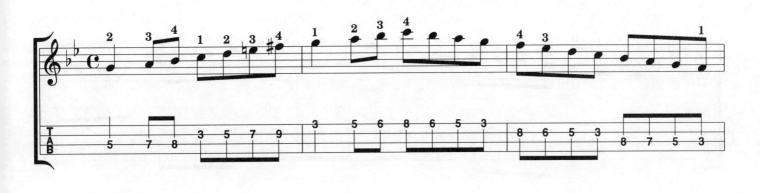

II Position F♯ Pure Minor Scale

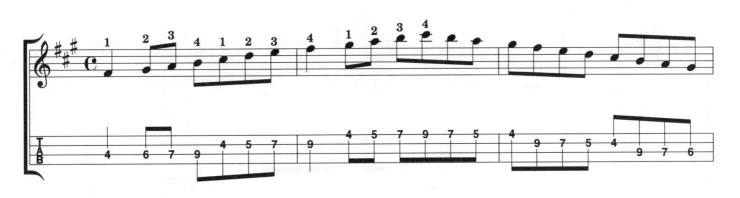

II Position F♯ Harmonic Minor Scale

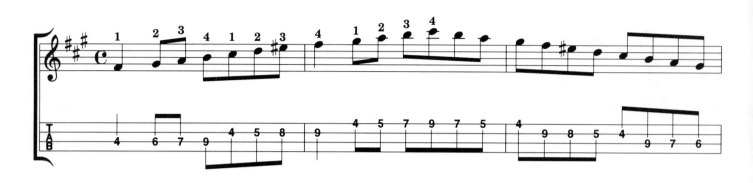

II Position F♯ Melodic Minor Scale

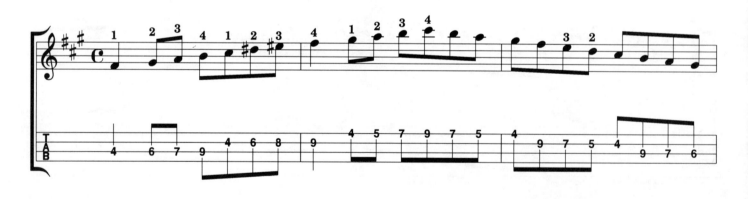

II Position C Pure Minor Scale

II Position C Harmonic Minor Scale

II Position C Melodic Minor Scale

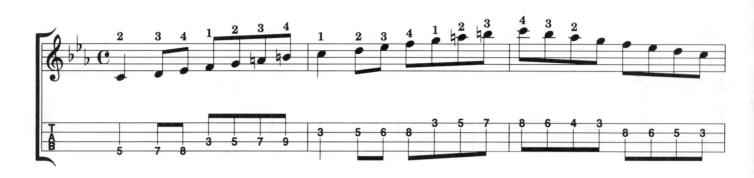

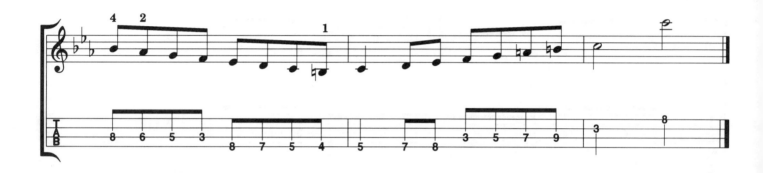

II Position C♯ Pure Minor Scale

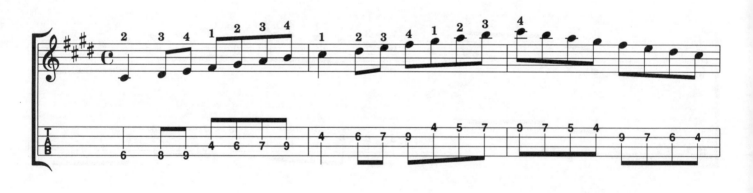

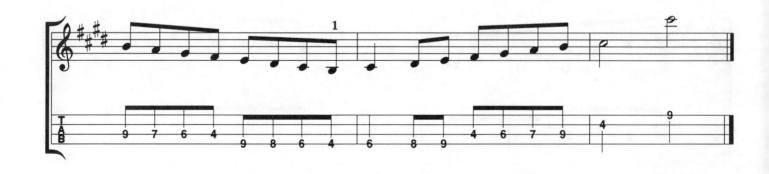

II Position C♯ Harmonic Minor Scale

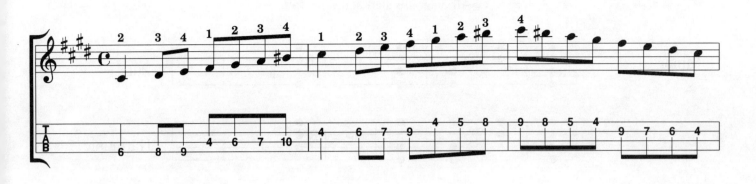

II Position C♯ Melodic Minor Scale

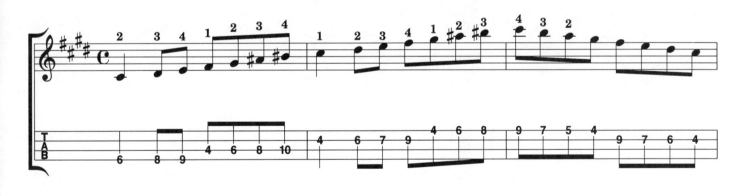

II Position Minor Scales

All diagrams start at the 3rd fret.

F Minor

Melodic diagram
is ascending only

G# Minor

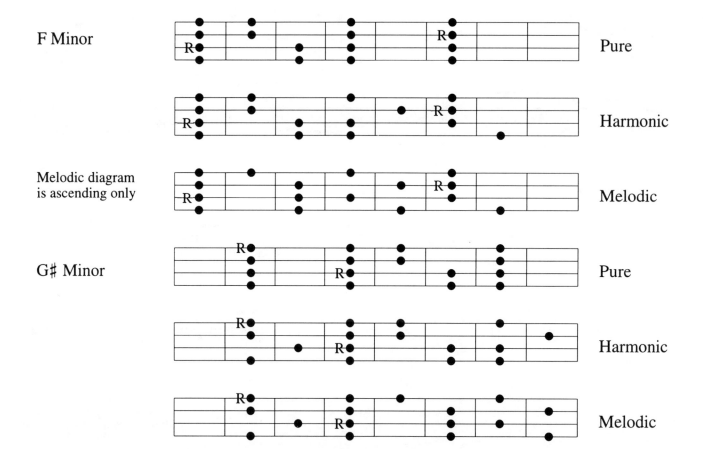

Pure

Harmonic

Melodic

Pure

Harmonic

Melodic

II Position F Pure Minor Scale

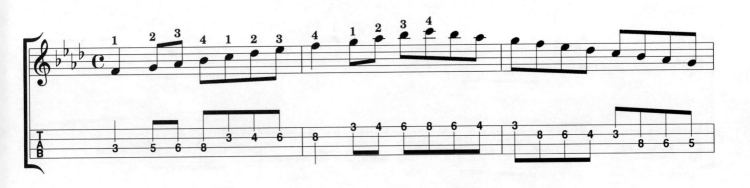

II Position F Harmonic Minor Scale

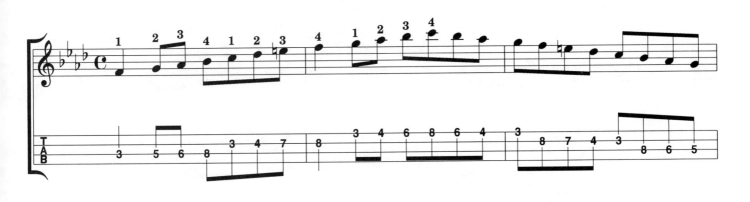

II Position F Melodic Minor Scale

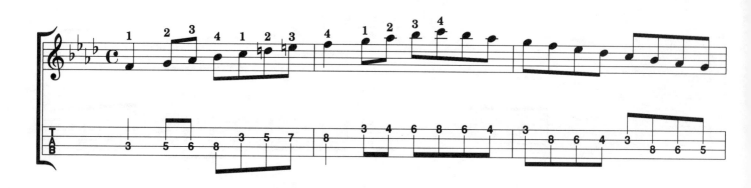

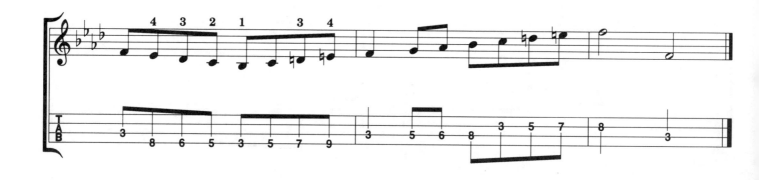

II Position G♯ Melodic Minor Scale

114

II Position G♯ Harmonic Minor Scale

II Position G♯ Melodic Minor Scale

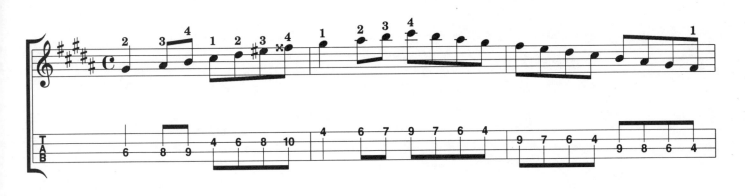

II Position Minor Scales

Diagrams start at the 2nd fret.

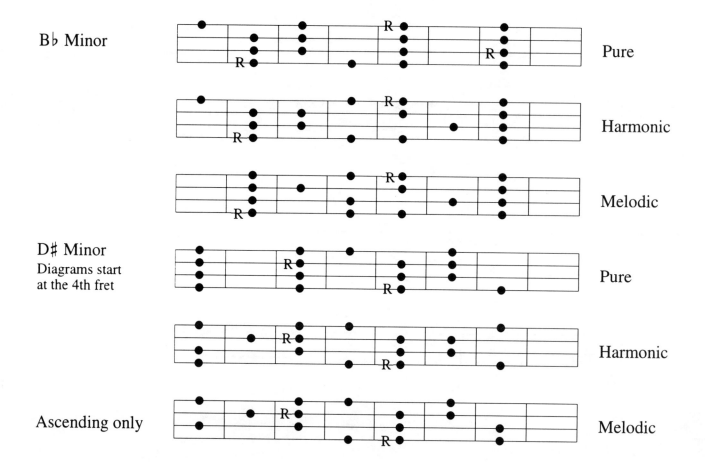

Bb Minor — Pure

Harmonic

Melodic

D# Minor
Diagrams start
at the 4th fret — Pure

Harmonic

Ascending only — Melodic

II Position B♭ Pure Minor Scale

II Position B♭ Harmonic Minor Scale

II Position B♭ Melodic Minor Scale

II Position D♯ Pure Minor Scale

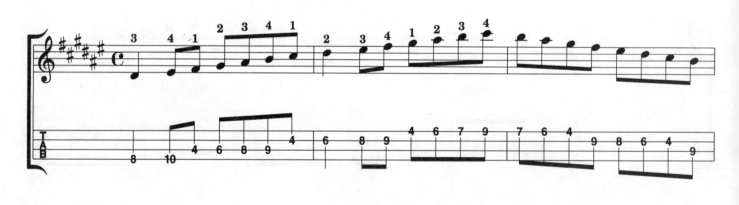

II Position D♯ Harmonic Minor Scale

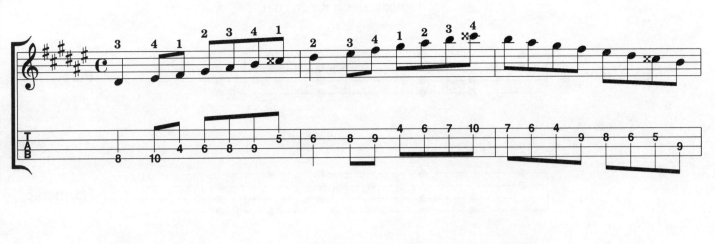

II Position D♯ Melodic Minor Scale

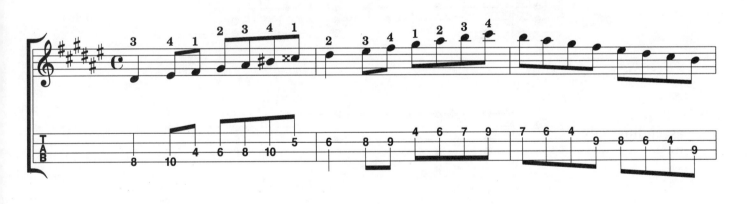

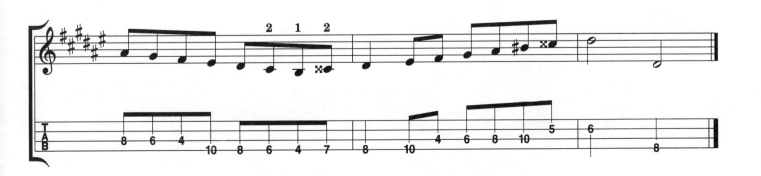

II Position Minor Scales
Diagrams start at the 2nd fret.

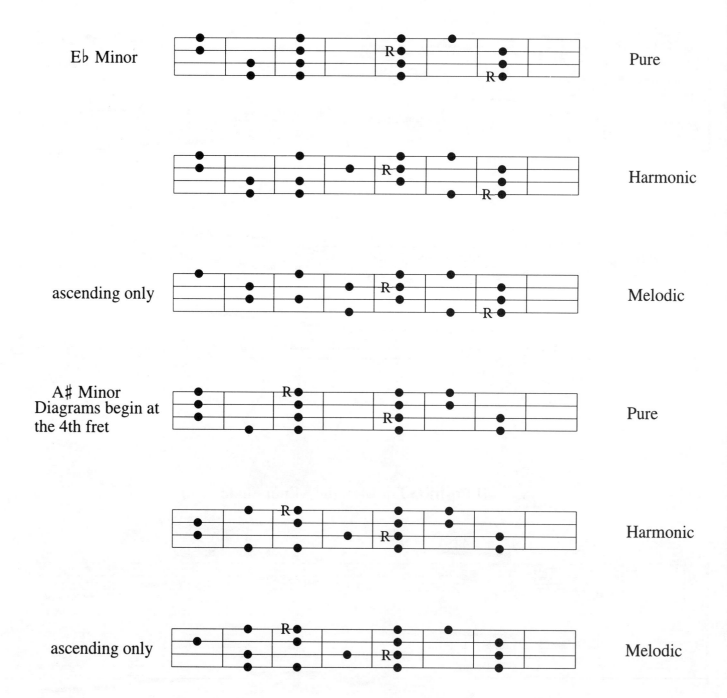

Eb Minor — Pure

Harmonic

ascending only — Melodic

A# Minor
Diagrams begin at
the 4th fret — Pure

Harmonic

ascending only — Melodic

II Position Eb Pure Minor Scale

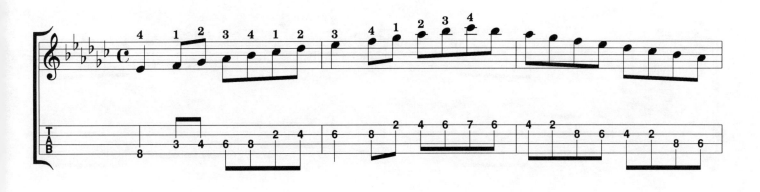

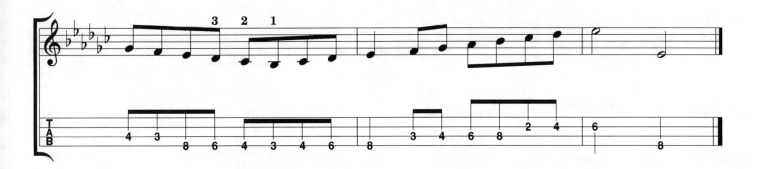

II Position Eb Harmonic Minor Scale

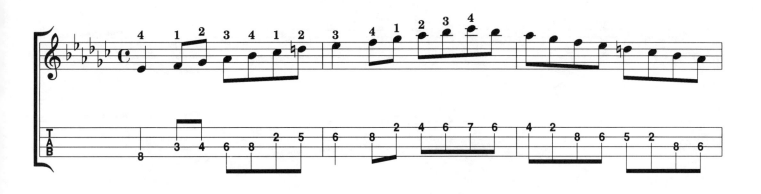

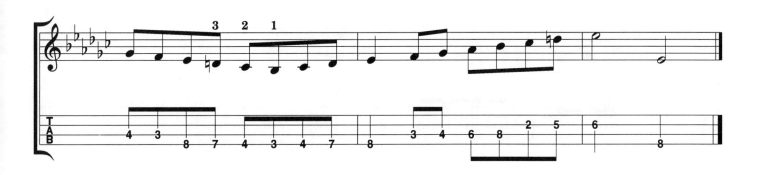

II Position E♭ Melodic Minor Scale

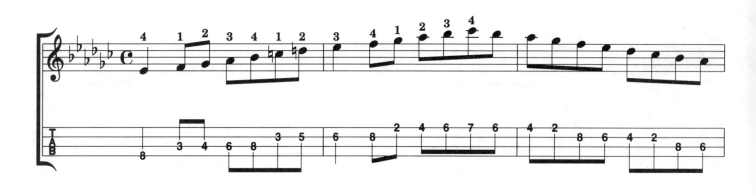

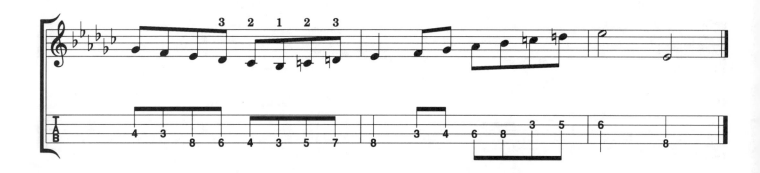

II Position A♯ Pure Minor Scale

II Position A♯ Harmonic Minor Scale

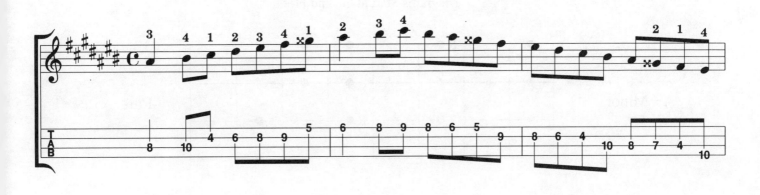

II Position A♯ Melodic Minor Scale

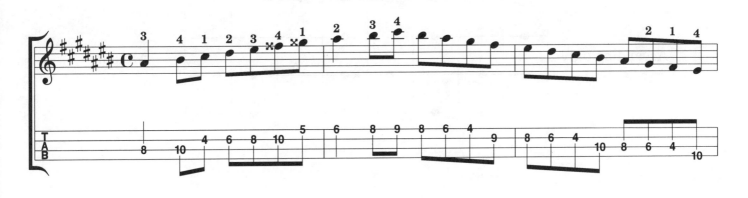

II Position Minor Scales
Diagrams Start at the 2nd Fret.

Ab Minor

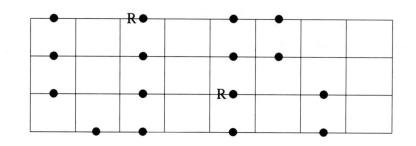

Pure

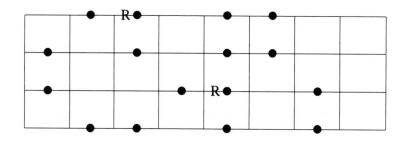

Harmonic

Ascending only

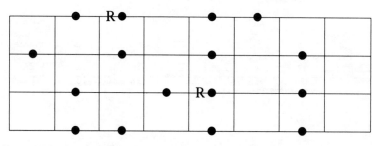

Melodic

II Position A♭ Pure Minor Scale

II Position A♭ Harmonic Minor Scale

II Position A♭ Melodic Minor Scale

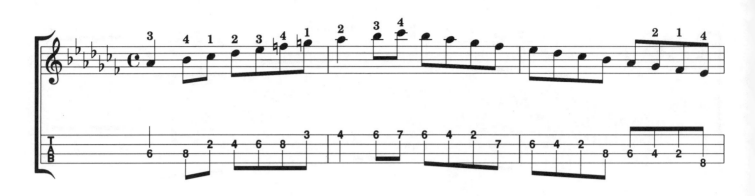

126

II Position C Chromatic Scale

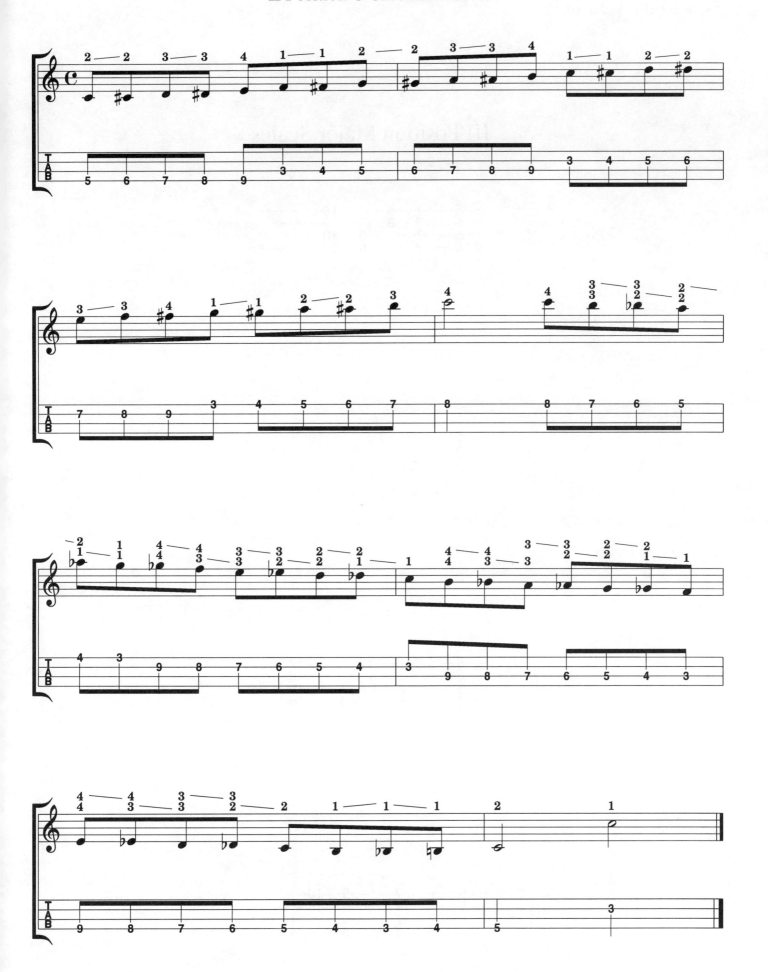

The next section deals with the III position. All of the available notes will be given in each key. The student should write scale exercises as desired.

III Position Major Scales

C

G
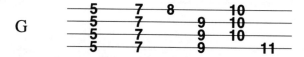

F
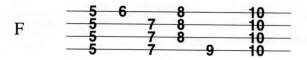

D
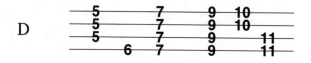

III Position C Scale

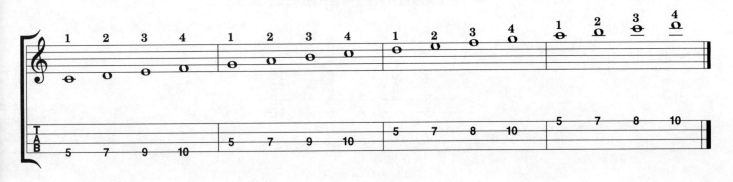

III Position G Major Scale

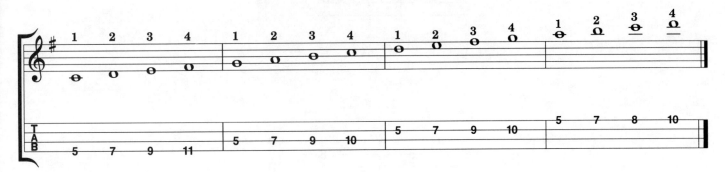

III Position F Major Scale

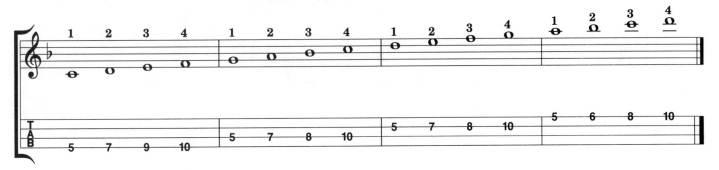

III Position D Major Scale

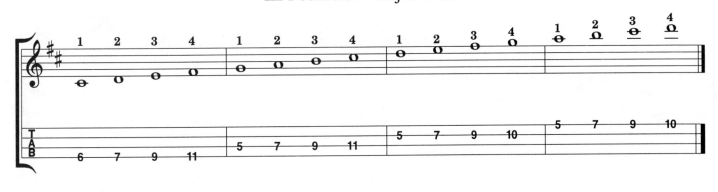

III Position Major Scales

B♭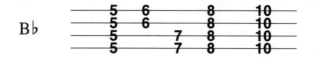

A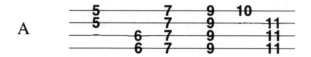

E♭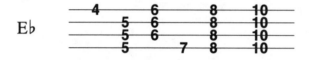

E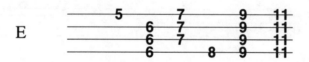

III Position B♭ Major Scale

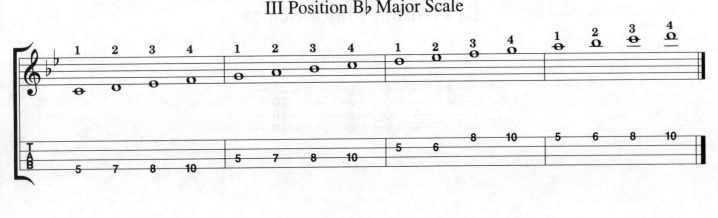

III Position A Major Scale

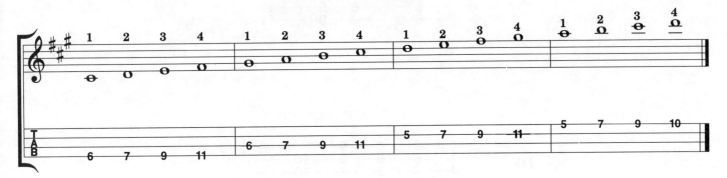

III Position E♭ Major Scale

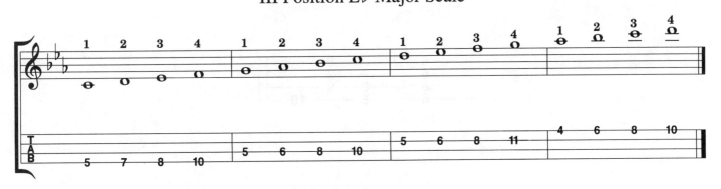

III Position E Major Scale

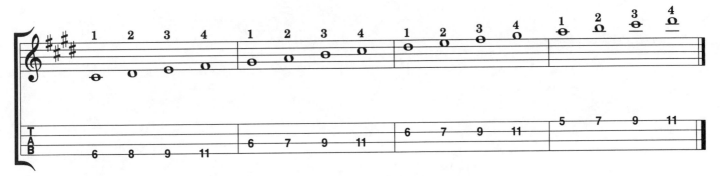

III Position Major Scales

Ab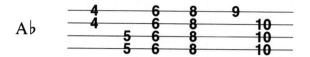

B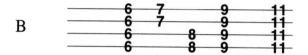

Db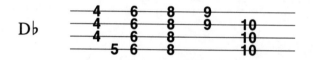

F#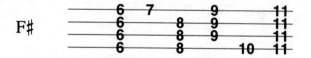

III Position A♭ Major Scale

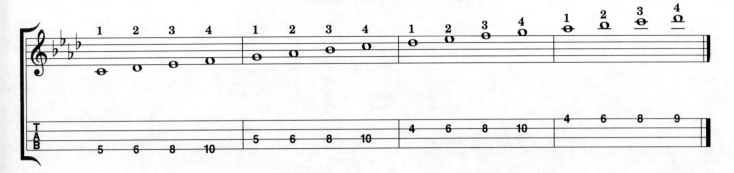

III Position B Major Scale

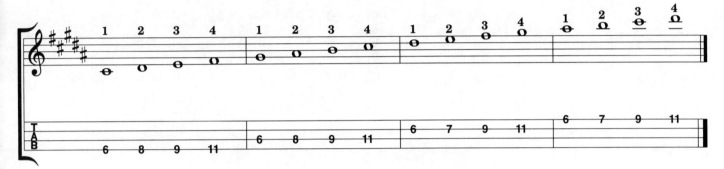

III Position D♭ Major Scale

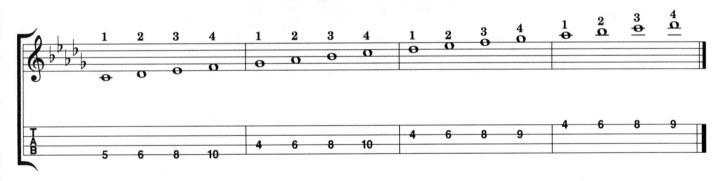

III Position F♯ Major Scale

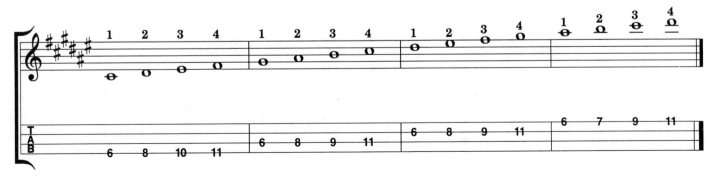

133

III Position Major Scales

Gb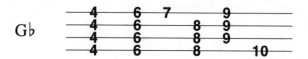

C#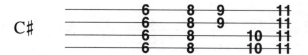

Cb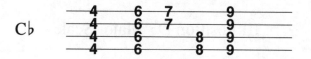

III Position G♭ Major Scale

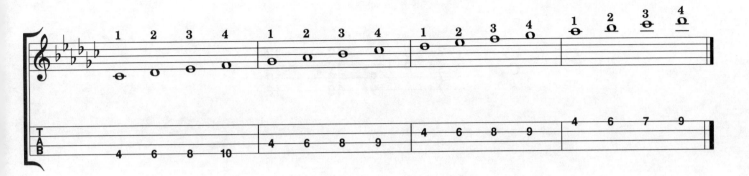

III Position C♯ Major Scale

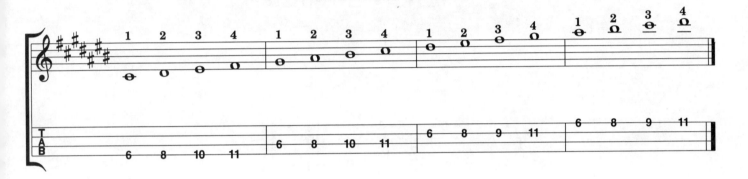

III Position C♭ Major Scale

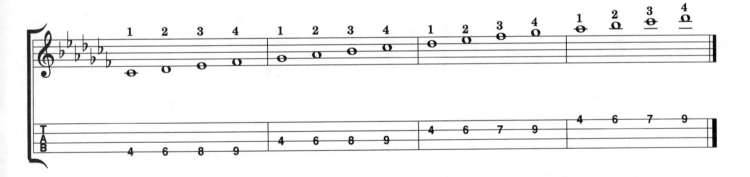

IV Position Major Scales

C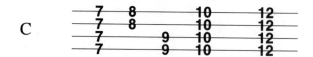

G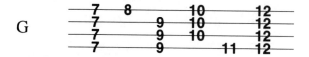

F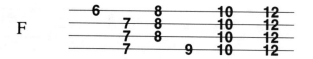

D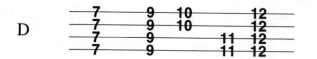

IV Position C Major Scale

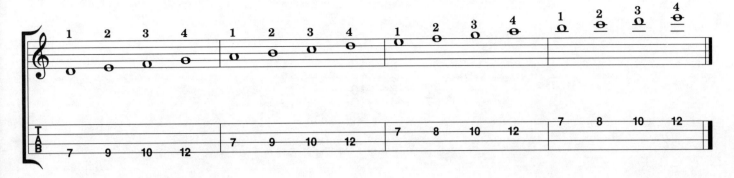

IV Position G Major Scale

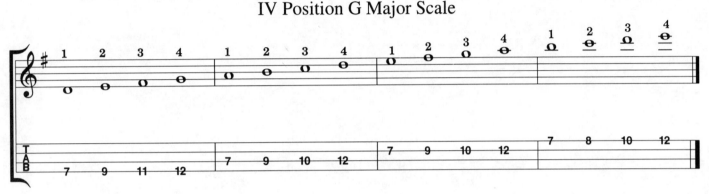

IV Position F Major Scale

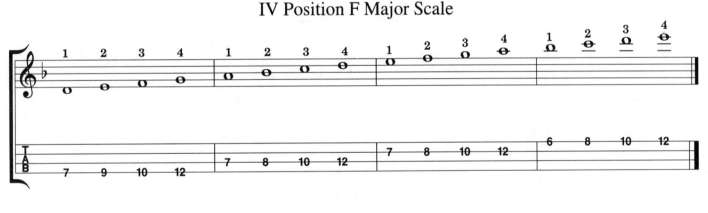

IV Position D Major Scale

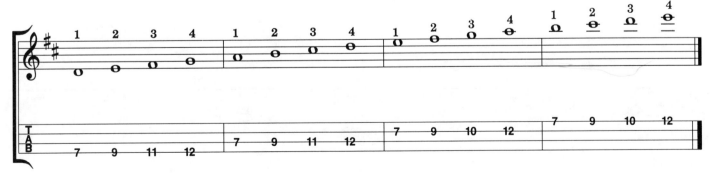

137

IV Position Major Scales

Bb
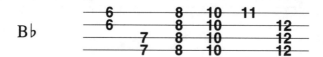

A
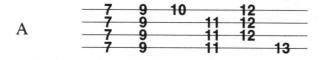

Eb
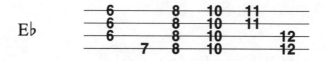

E
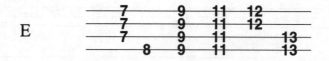

IV Position B♭ Major Scale

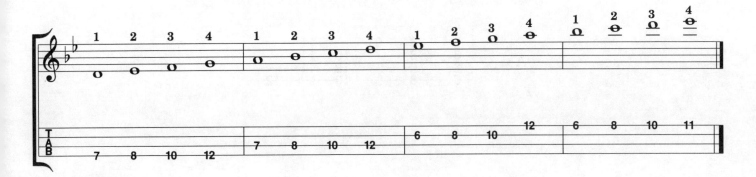

IV Position A Major Scale

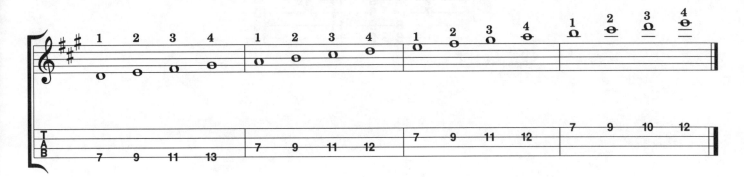

IV Position E♭ Major Scale

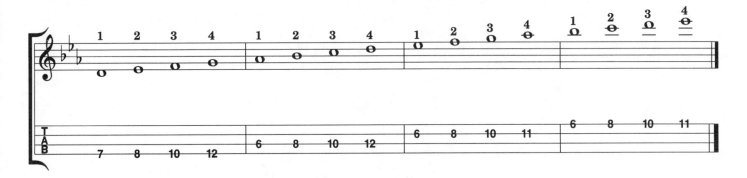

IV Position E Major Scale

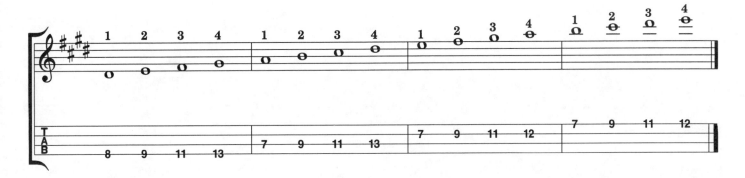

IV Position Major Scales

A♭
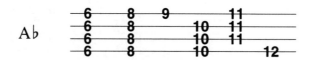

B
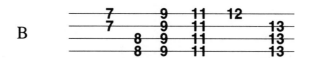

D♭
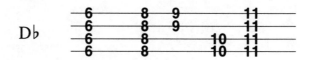

F♯
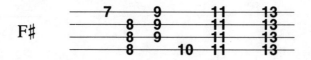

IV Position A♭ Major Scale

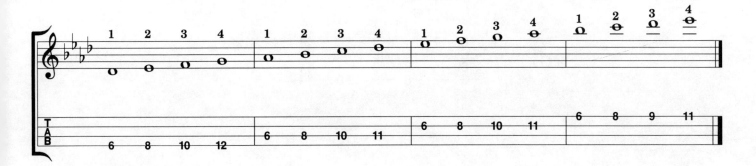

IV Position B Major Scale

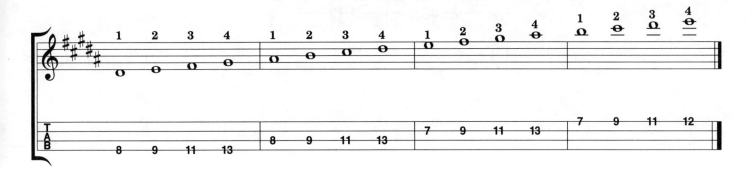

IV Position D♭ Major Scale

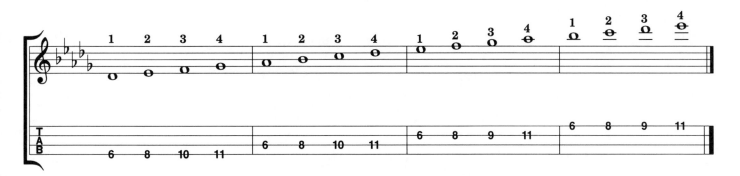

IV Position F♯ Major Scale

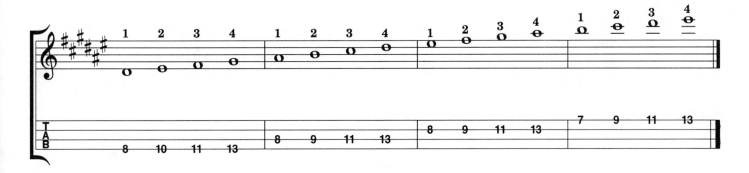

IV Position Major Scales

Gb
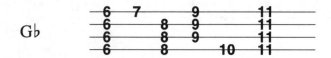

C#
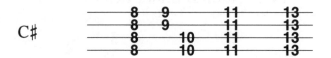

Cb
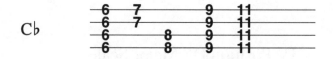

IV Position G♭ Major Scale

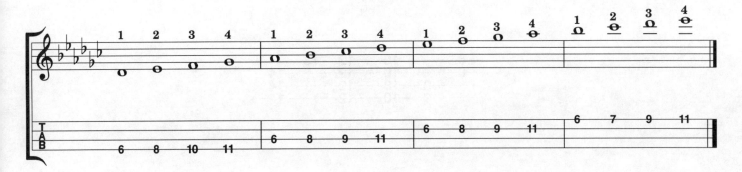

IV Position C♯ Major Scale

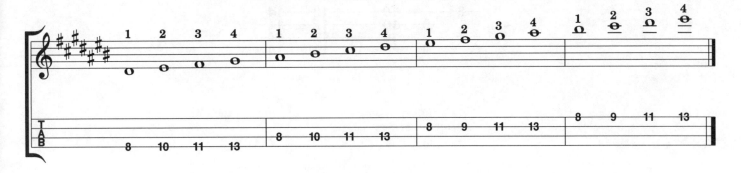

IV Position C♭ Major Scale

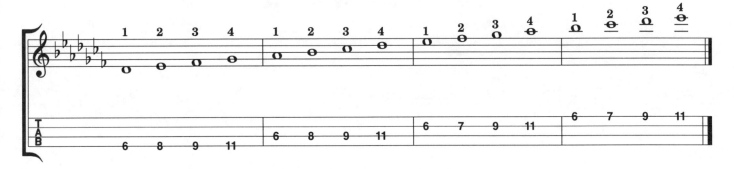

V Position Major Scales

C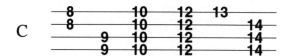

G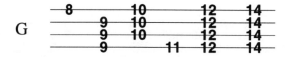

F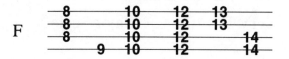

D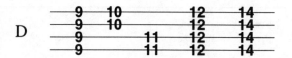

V Position C Major Scale

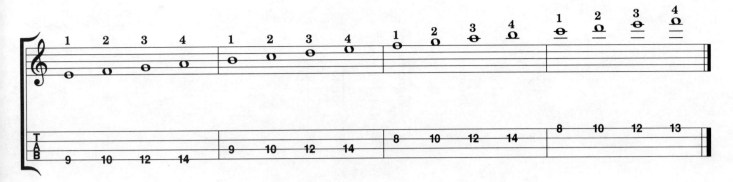

V Position G Major Scale

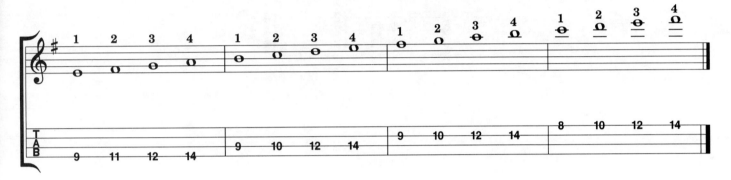

V Position F Major Scale

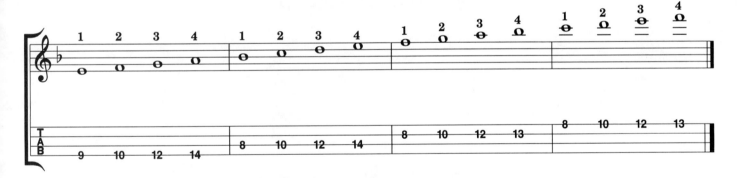

V Position D Major Scale

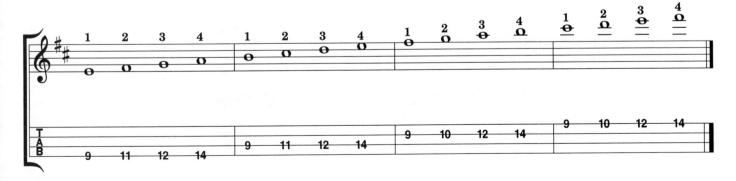

V Position Major Scales

Bb

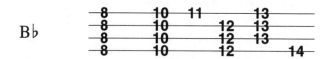

A

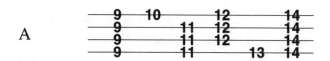

Eb

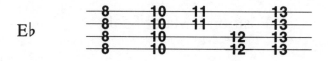

E

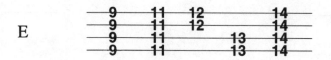

V Position B♭ Major Scale

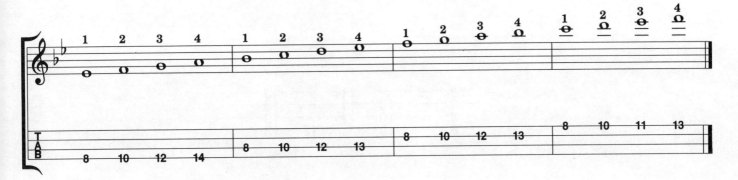

V Position A Major Scale

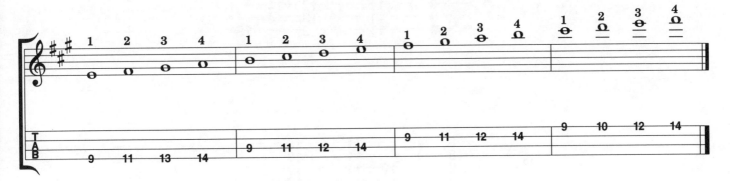

V Position E♭ Major Scale

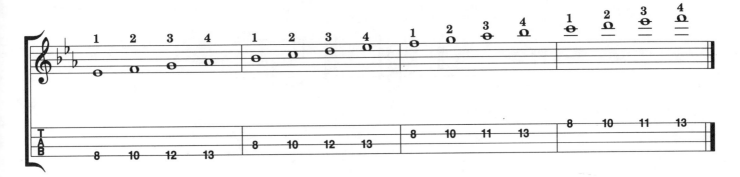

V Position E Major Scale

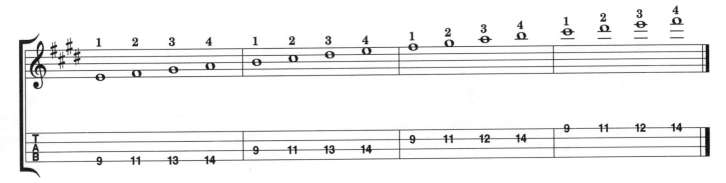

147

V Position Major Scales

Ab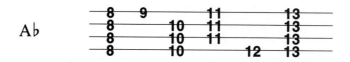

B

Db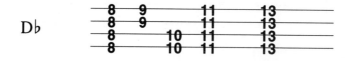

F#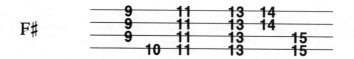

148

V Position A♭ Major Scale

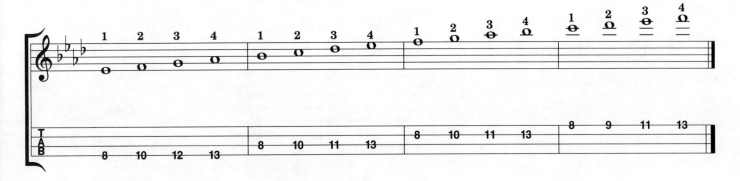

V Position B Major Scale

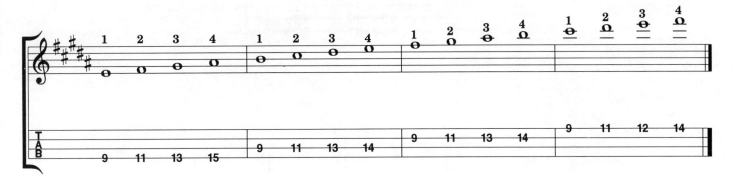

V Position D♭ Major Scale

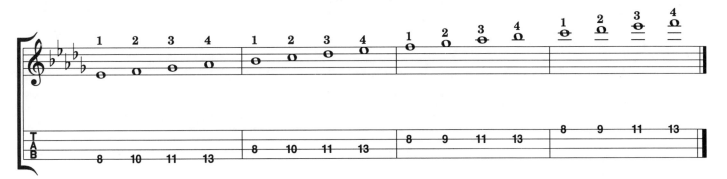

V Position F♯ Major Scale

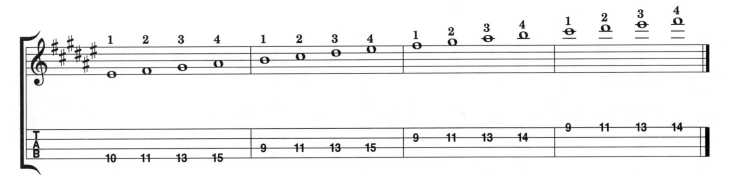

V Position Major Scales

Gb

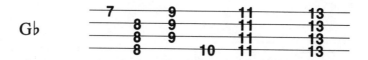

C#

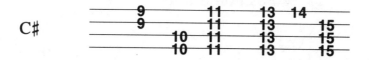

Cb

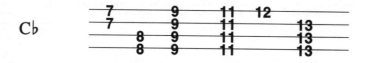

V Position Gb Major Scale

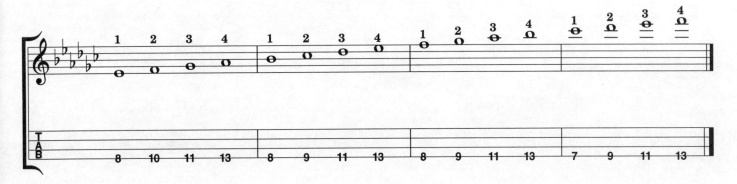

V Position C# Major Scale

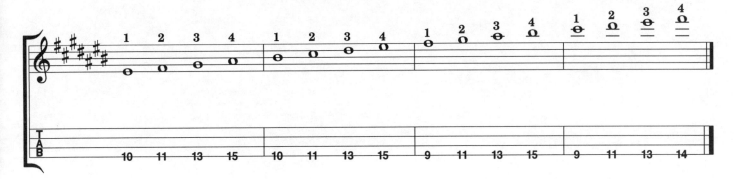

V Position Cb Major Scale

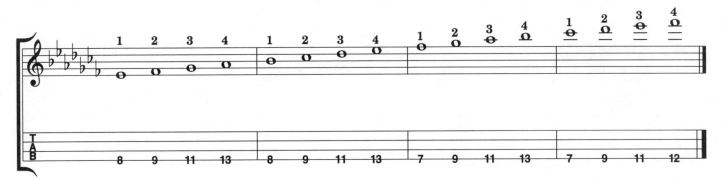

151